Praise for Mr. Hamlin's List

"... a wonderfully told tale of wealth, passion, love, and family loyalty all wrapped up in a historical novel about the Cripple Creek & Victor Labor Wars of 1903-04. Nice read and great historical context."

—Ruth Zalewski, Director,
Victor Lowell Thomas Museum

... an accurate telling of a dramatic bloody day in Colorado history.

... well lays out the violent, seamy side of life in the 'Greatest Gold Camp on Earth.'

... a little known chapter of America's labor strife, with a personal connection to the author.

General Pearson's Ship

Other Books by Stan Moore

Over the Dam
Mik Mas uncovers and works to stop eco-vigilantes in today's Summit County, Colorado.
Fiction (overthedam.com)

Seesaw: How November '42 Shaped the Future
A fresh look at the crux month of WWII.
Nonfiction (seesaw1942.com)

Mister Moffat's Road
A historical novel about David Moffat's railroad from Denver towards Salt Lake City, set in 1902. Mik Mas and friends help Moffat to overcome unforeseen barriers.

Mister Moffat's Hill
A historical novel, 1904–08 Colorado.
Cam Braun and Mik Mas struggle to run trains over the continental divide's Rollins Pass. A diamond mine scheme comes to their attention and fireworks result.

Mister Moffat's Opus
A historical novel set in 1917–1929 Colorado. Political maneuvering and financial shenanigans underlie the Moffat Tunnel railroad project. It took five years to build, cost millions, and was the largest construction project in the nation. Mik Mas and Cam Braun are in the thick of the effort.

Mister Hamlin's List
A historical novel set in 1900s Cripple Creek, the 'Greatest Gold Camp on Earth.' Follow Ben McNall, a union miner who falls for a woman mine owner. There is violence between the union, owners, strike breakers and the Colorado Militia. Ultimately many people leave town, some voluntarily and some are deported.

General Pearson's Ship

Stan Moore

This is a work of historical fiction. Events occurred as described and the story was given life by word and action of the fictional characters.

Many people contributed to this work. At the risk of not naming everyone, I want to thank my cousin Bill Robinson for the initial inspiration. Cherry Moore, Robert Ticknor and Phil Homan offered historical and research insights. My wife Kiki Moore, as ever, offered advice, encouragement, and the book's cover.

Errors and oversights, hopefully few, are mine alone.

© 2022 Stan Moore

All rights reserved. No part of this book may be reproduced or transmitted in any form or by any means, electronic or mechanical, including photocopying, recording, or by an information storage and retrieval system—except by a reviewer who may quote brief passages in a review—without permission in writing from the publisher.

Design by Jack Lenzo

This book is dedicated to the hundreds of thousands of
horses and mules on both sides.
They loyally fought, lived and died in
their owners' Boer War, 1899–1902.

Contents

Cast of Characters and Events xi

I	"Copernicus Oursa…	1
II	Across town…	9
III	Licia sat ahorse…	17
IV	The man's British accent…	23
V	"Specialize? My specialty is…	31
VI	Cope set the pad…	37
VII	The newcomer's British accent…	43
VIII	Licia perused the menu…	49
IX	As Licia stood…	55
X	Gace was drinking in…	63
XI	Holding the 'grams…	71
XII	Cope ambled almost…	79
XIII	'REDCOAT INVASION!'	85
XIV	The café was half…	93
XV	Ted Moore stood…	99
XVI	"…but yours too."	107
XVII	Gace didn't know what…	113
XVIII	The hostler paused…	119
XIX	"Will you help me?	123
XX	Cope needed to get…	127
XXI	The closer the man came…	133
XXII	"Tell me again Cope.	137

XXIII	Later. Licia relived… 143
XXIV	Life's daily rhythms returned… 147
XXV	Cope wandered home, 151
XXVI	The quiet in her office… 155
XXVII	Gace and Licia took… 165
XXVIII	Cope paused, took in the crazy… 171
XXIX	The next day went in fits… 179
XXX	Cope was pleasantly surprised… 185
XXXI	Cope sidled along the… 195

Afterword 199
About the Author 201

Cast of Characters and Events

THE SECOND ANGLO BOER WAR, 1899–1902
This conflict was fought in southern Africa around the turn of the twentieth century. It was the closing act of a decades old conflict between British imperial forces and citizen guerillas. Boers were farmers and independent traders who had lived there from the 1600s. Descended from Dutch, German and French settlers, they were proudly and jealously independent. The British had been extending their empire to southern Africa bit by bit. The late 1800's discovery of gold and diamonds brought matters to a boil. The two sides fought, neither giving or taking quarter; the British involved the Boer populace in the mayhem. Neither gave much consideration to the native population. Each would use, make common cause with, or fight the various tribes as expedient.

WHO IS WHO
Historical characters. These persons lived the times and are realistically portrayed:

Samuel Pearson. An American activist who acts as a General in Boer forces even though he spent the war years in the United States.

Bill Haywood. A miners' union executive and activist.

Charles Owens. Irish by birth, he is an eastern Colorado rancher, happy to sell horses and mules at the right price.

Katherine Moore. House manager at the Owens Ranch. She too is Irish by birth.

Ted Moore. A ranch hand, Katherine's son.

OTHERS
Copernicus (goes by Cope) Oursa. Elder son in a Boer family, working as a reporter for a Pretoria newspaper, De Volksstem.

George Armstrong Custer McNall (goes by Gace) an ex silver miner, works as a livestock buyer/contractor.

Felicity Heldon (answers to Licia) is Colorado ranch raised. She is back from a year in the east and works in the emerging animal welfare industry.

Paul Piers-Read. British Army officer and horseman.

Ella Queue. A longtime Denver animal rights activist.

Cam Braun. A railroad executive.

I

"Copernicus Oursa, U.S. Correspondent." Cam Braun's gravelly voice drew out the name on the business card. His raised eyebrows and unstated question caught his guest off guard.

"Oursa. That is an interesting name. What is your background?"

The business card dropped onto the desk and Cam waited for a response. The man's mild expression went against the gravelly voice and persona the guest had already started to construct. Cam smiled kindly, patient for his visitor's answer.

The man behind the desk looked big, tall, heavy. The huge hands made the business card look like a postage stamp. The impression one first had of Cam was almost of a street tough.

But the visitor knew better. He was sitting in front of his desk in a private office not far from David Moffat's suite. In a fancy Seventeenth Street Denver bank. There were clerks silent gliding on mysterious errands and the smell of money wafted heavily in the air. Apparently Cam had something going besides physical strength. The guest stuffed such thoughts and replied, smiling as well.

"Call me Cope, please. Not Copernicus. I only heard that from my mother when I was in trouble. Besides, it is long and doesn't roll off the tongue!"

He chuckled to himself, remembering his mother summoning him, eyes ablaze at some childly sin.

"Actually the name Oursa is of the French. It is a corruption of the French word 'ours.'" Cope had a hunch the big guy knew more than he let on, and grinned. "So bear with me."

Cam groaned. "Ours, as I remember from my scattered reading, means bear." So you're from Africa, right, not France?"

Cope nodded and grinned as he decided it would be a job to stay up with this guy. Physically and mentally.

"Yes, 'ours' means 'bear.' My heritage is Huguenot—the Protestants who were kicked out of French territories in the 1600s. Some French Canadians ended up in your Louisiana. My people left France—in a hurry, with little—and put down roots in southern Africa. They melded with Dutch and Germans already settled there. The result of that melting pot, with a little native blood stirred in, is the Boers."

Cope figured the short version was enough, and it was.

Cam's eyes became unfocused. This story brought to mind his people's saga.

"Ah. Some of my forebears came from Africa."

This was said almost dreamily. Then Cam looked sharply at his visitor but his voice remained without hard edges or definite intonation.

"It was not a trip they took to improve their lives. They were kidnapped and sold to slave traders by rival tribes. Some of those traders in human flesh were European, some Arabs, and some were native Africans. In any case, my ancestors ended up here, in North America. Over time they too melded with Germans and many others. I am the American product."

His eyes refocused and his voice changed from wistful to businesslike.

"But you didn't come to hear about that."

The visitor smiled and nodded. The gesture held empathy and energy.

"So, Mister Braun. I'm sure you know that we Boers live and die by our horses. We are farmers and small townsmen. Our Velds are like your Great Plains. They are huge, with boundless skies, and seem to go on forever. Like your prairies, they are usually friendly and fruitful. Of course at times life there is unforgiving and hostile. Since they are wide and empty a man can't get around without a good animal."

Cam nodded, having in fact just ridden a stretch of railroad, on horse. He was Mister Moffat's eyes and ears; from time to time he just went out and observed. He had been out on one of those trips.

Cope didn't pause, just went on.

"In fact without a good horse you are helpless and in danger. From an early age, almost before I could walk, I was put on a horse. I tell you so you see I know horses and their value."

Braun nodded. "First, call me Cam, none of the 'mister' stuff. And yes, horses have been the lifeblood and remain important to our nation and economy. But. Now here in the States, the railroad is taking the place of horses in many ways. Here, you still need a horse to get around town or the farm. You need one for local work. If you want to travel far, fast and safely, go to the train."

"Just so, Cam. And my editor's assignment is for me to learn how you use animals in building your railroad. Ironic, isn't it, you use horses to make them obsolete?"

As Cope asked that he had a flash image of his editor. The man also told him to find out about the US horse trade generally.

Braun nodded at the irony. His job title was railroad foreman. He had worked for David Moffat's road through the mountains. These days he found himself not supervising crews, rather overseeing the operations generally. And acting as a troubleshooter.

Cam man was curious and knowledgeable; when he could get one, he always wanted a first hand account. He knew that newspapers' and other observers weren't totally inaccurate. Yet they seldom told the whole story. Rather than answer Cope's question he posed one of his own.

"And now your Boers are in a struggle there in southern Africa. From what I read it sounds a brawl." He added, "And I bet the native people are caught in the middle of it, like it or not."

This last sounded like an afterthought but it was not; he had visceral sympathy for innocent bystanders. The term 'collateral damage' hadn't been invented but he was familiar with the concept.

Cope was a little taken aback at the veer to a new subject. He thought a moment before responding.

"Yes. Yes to both. My family and neighbors fight the British. They keep coming, more and more troops and guns. The natives are caught up like you say. Friends I grew up with, native boys, are now scattered worse than the Boers. Everything and everyone are thrown to the wind. Everything is overturned and up for grabs, which is saying something." He paused, his mind suddenly thousands of miles away.

"But back to my work here in Denver Colorado. I was sent here to observe and report on animal practices here in the US. And on the animal industry in its bits and pieces. America is nice and all, and I enjoy the work."

He himself veered back to the Boers.

"But I miss my family and my country. I wish more than anything that I could go out on Commando and help kill Engelse."

He didn't notice that he spoke his native Afrikaans language as he spat the word for 'English' or 'Englishmen.'

Braun raised an inquiring eyebrow. "First a French name, now another language?"

"English, I want to go kill Englishmen. Or at least drive them away. We want nothing but to be left alone to run our farms and be independent."

Cam nodded, saying nothing.

"But I have a job to do here. The editors of my paper, De Volksstem, are paying me to tell the world about your animals, your modern railroads and how you build them."

Cope grinned sourly, mind back again in Africa.

"Actually they—De Volksstem and her editors—will likely be shut down by the British if they take Pretoria. Or when they take Pretoria—any day now I expect that to happen. Thankfully the editors have Dutch backers and they will work to find a way to keep publishing. But enough about the war."

Braun chuckled mirthlessly.

"The politicians sure love their wars, don't they? Our leaders have been busy sending troops to Hawaii and Cuba and the Philippines and Guam and God knows where else. The Russians and Japanese are glowering over Manchuria. They'll be fighting soon, you watch. And Chinese, or at least a sect called the Boxers, are working themselves up to expel or kill Christians and westerners. Not to mention the Brits and their wars up in Egypt and the Sudan, and Nigeria in West Africa. It makes you wonder…"

"Yes, just so. There are always wars going on. But back to business. Tell me, Mr. Braun…"

"Cam, please."

"Yes. Tell me, Cam, about animals and building your railroad through the Rockies. And under them, for that matter. Are they used underground, in building tunnels? Or to supply the forward parties, the surveyors and loggers and so on? How many hostlers and horse crews do you keep? Tell me about it."

Many questions and answers later, Cope glanced at the clock. Time to go.

"Thank you for your time, Cam. It has been most interesting."

With a grin, "I'm happy to do it, Mr. Oursa."

"Call me Cope. Copernicus, Cope."

"Sure, Cope. If you want to come visit a work camp at end of tracks, where the horses and mules earn their oats, let me know. We can take you into the wild and put you up for a few days. We might even see a bear!" He grinned and went on, "Seriously, we can arrange a tour. I need to get out myself, go see what is really happening. I will act as your tour guide!"

"Thank you, Cam. That sounds interesting and informative. So yes, I would like to see the working end of a railroad. I will be in touch to set that up. Let me clear it with the editor and check my calendar. What, a trip of three or four days? Is that alright?"

He stood, extending his hand with a smile. "Good bye, Cam."

Gathering his notes, he put them is his case. He noticed a letter from home he had stuck in earlier. In the rush to get to the interview he thought to read it later. The envelope arrived just before he left to meet Braun. Reading the address in his mother's handwriting made him anxious to see the news. It had been quite a while since he had word from home. He took it out, intending to open it and read as soon as he could.

On the street he found a bench, sat and looked again at her handwriting. It seemed a little shaky or was that his imagination? He hoped she had good things to say, so ripped into it.

At the first words, his world started to unravel. It was all he could do to hold on, sit up and not drop the letter. The message was short and small but the news was huge. It was too big, too bad.

> Dear son. I have nothing good to tell. Your father, out on Commando, was shot and killed. Not sure where the fight nor where he is buried. The Engelse then came on to our farm. Turned our stock loose then shot and butchered a cow. After they burned the farmhouse. I give this to a friend to send and hope it gets to you. We are being sent to a camp, one of the British 'concentration camps.' Will write as I can.

Cope held on to the letter, barely, and his arm went limp in his lap.

Eyes vacant, he stared down Seventeenth Street, Denver's busy financial hub. He did not see trolley cars or building strung with electric wires. He didn't see anything modern or urban or crowded.

Rather he saw wide open space. It was his native veld with its grassy rolling plains. He remembered, cherished the image of his home farm. His own horse. He imagined word coming to his father, someone riding up alone with a message, an order. The dreaded order to go on Commando.

Father was a peaceful man and the need to go hunt and shoot others would have disturbed him. But he knew he had to defend his home and way of life, so he went. His wife, dutifully, would have gathered a week's worth or more of food, into a bag. In his mind's eye, Cope saw his father take the bag, embrace her, climb on his horse.

What went through his mother's mind as her mate rode away? He imagined the woman who birthed him as she stood, watching. Watching as her man got smaller and smaller, clad in brownish gray with a big hat, food bag tied to the saddle and holstered rifle. He was off to meet other men, neighbors and friends. They would find and repel the British invaders. Drive off the Engelse, the men who wanted to deprive them of home, family and life. The invaders had to be defeated.

Somehow it went wrong, and Father was killed. Maybe others were too, Cope didn't know. But he did know that some troops, probably those who killed his father, came and burnt the farm. He envisioned his mother trying to shelter his siblings and save what supplies and possessions she could. And he tried not to picture the British soldiers forcing his family to a camp.

Cope was overcome. He sat and sat, unable to think or move. After a while, not sure how long, clarity started to come. He had to do something, anything, to help them. Somehow.

II

Across town, near the Denver railroad yards, it was just everyday business. This was the busy spot where animals were brought in for trade and husbandry. Many were shipped on to eastern markets for slaughter. Here no men sat, reeling, enraged and feeling guilty. No one was concerned with a war between two distant countries. Truth be known, people cared chiefly about their own concerns and lives. Unless a son or father was involved, little attention was paid even to wars waged by their own government.

The corrals were full: the cattle, sheep, horses and pigs made their noises and odors, getting on or off trains or just milling around in pens. Nearby, the Stockyards Inn was busy as usual. This fine old food and drink institution was cheek to jowl with corrals and loading chutes. The Inn was the epicenter of the ranching and farming business. The influential and powerful people who frequented the place didn't dress like the Seventeenth Street crowd. That said, the Stetson and denim crowd easily wielded as much influence as the buttoned down financiers.

Gace McNall always enjoyed dropping in at the 'Yards. It was fun to see and be seen. Catch up on the livestock business. Make deals and get gossip. It was a fine way to get some perspective on life in general. Today, he wasn't just hanging out, seeing who was doing what to whom. No, today he had a meeting. It was in follow up of a good lead.

The sun was big and sky deep blue, a nice day. After he stepped in it took a moment for his eyes to adjust. Inside was lit well enough to see and safely cut your steak and potatoes, but not bright and airy. Gace scanned the room and his eyes gradually adjusted; the view came clear. The man he was to meet, at least Gace figured him to be the one, sat across the room. He headed that way. As he went, words of greeting floated up.

"Hullo Gace." "Hey, horse man, how's business?" "Jeez, McNall, I guess they'll let anyone in here!" Making fairly slow progress, he bantered with stockmen, traders, and the occasional banker. Greetings and catcalls came from friends and associates, or friendly competitors. Some silently shot him daggered looks. As usual when an old pro came in, many in the room were greeting or good naturedly jeering. Gace loved it. He gave as good as he got. Soon enough he reached the corner where his man sat, morose and looking lonely, sipping coffee.

Gace stopped, held out his hand, smiled. "Mr. Read? I'm Gace McNall. Nice to meet you."

The man stood, ramrod straight, almost as if coming to attention. He smiled through his thick British accent and took the offered hand. His British accent was picturesquely out of place in a ranching tavern.

"Paul Piers-Read. Nice to meet you. You seem well known in here. Gace, you say?"

They sat; Gace motioned for the waiter to bring him coffee and warm up Paul's.

"Yeah, this is kind of livestock central here in Denver." He added cream but let the coffee sit.

"Gace, yes, it is an unusual name." He smiled again. "My full moniker is George Armstrong Custer McNall. My parents took the traditional route of naming us kids for famous people, in hopes we'd emulate them. I hated being a George so I soon adopted Gace from the initials. It stuck."

"Well, I hope you don't emulate the man too closely. His life was a bright flair but short."

Gace regarded the man. He was a Brit, and scuttlebutt had him an army officer, Royal Army. But he apparently knew something of American history. Did the guy know horses, was the question.

"Well, I have no intention of living or dying the way he did. No battlefield heroics for me, thank you very much. Not even a uniform or a salute, not me." He emphasized this with a vigorous negative shake of his head. "As a youngster I avoided the Army. Came west and mined silver. I loved the work, the camaraderie. I loved being in and inside the mountains, wresting wealth from Mother Earth. Not to mention living and enjoying the fine full throttle towns."

"Once a silver miner now a horse trader. There has to be a story there."

"There is, a common one. I did well with it until the Crash of '93."

He took a sip of coffee, grimaced. "Jeez, today they must have reused the dishwater." He shoved the cup away and went on. Looked at Read inquiringly.

"You know the Crash of '93?"

Piers-Read had an idea, but wasn't sure. He was curious. "Not really. Tell me."

"The government had been buying a guaranteed amount silver every month. Millions of ounces. They were backing the Dollar with both gold and silver, I am told. But I'm the first to admit that financial talk is over my head." He tried a fresh cup of coffee the waiter brought by. It was better.

"Anyway, in the 1880's and early 90's, silver miners and mine owners and smelters were in tall clover. But one day the money dried up. Just ended. The guaranteed purchases from Washington stopped. No warning, at least not to us underground working stiffs. The millionaires probably saw it coming but we didn't. Overnight, me and thousands of others were out of work. Silver mining towns dried up. Aspen, Leadville, Carson City, Silverton, other places went dark. In a matter of days or weeks."

The Brit nodded, spreading his hands, a curiously sympathetic gesture.

"Yes, I remember reading about it. I was in Japan at the time, military attache. Read every English language paper I could lay my hands on. And I watched the Japanese prepare to defeat the Chinese. Which they did in '94 and '95, so I lost track of finance in America. They, the Emperor's men, occupied part of the mainland. Mainland China! And took on, defeated, the Russians! We Europeans—and that means you Americans too—need to pay attention. I tell you, look out for those Sons of the Emperor. They are on the march. But I digress."

"No, please go on. That is interesting. I've never been to Asia, would love to see it. You have a military background then?"

"Yes. Joined up as a lad of fifteen and the Army has treated me well. I have traveled and met many fine people and had many interesting jobs. Have seen bullets fly, thank God they flew right by me. But that is for young men to experience. Now I am purchasing officer for the western US."

Piers-Read wanted to deflect. He learned more, did better, when asking questions rather than answering them.

"So you were suddenly an ex-miner. How did you come to meet a Royal Army purchasing officer in the horse business in Colorado?"

"Well, Paul, its like this. I have a brother, a gold miner, name of Ben. Benjamin Franklin McNall don't you know. He too got dumped out of silver but he found work in the goldfields. He is down in Cripple." He glanced and saw no recognition, rather curiosity.

"Cripple?"

"Cripple Creek. It is a gold mining town down south. Named by a rancher who had a calf with a broken leg caught up in a barbed wire fence. Anyway the place is rich as Croesus, calls itself 'the greatest gold camp on earth.'

"Men in the Yukon might disagree! Not to mention South Africa."

"Yeah, probably so. Anyway. Cripple. It is located about a hundred miles south and west of us. Down west of Pikes Peak, high in an old volcanic crater. I liked mining a lot then, just after '93. My thought was to have him, brother Ben, help get me on there. He has connections with the union and some owners. I actually went down and looked things over. It is quite a gold camp, running and gunning, literally."

Gace took a wary swallow of coffee, thinking of the gold mines.

"Whew, Paul. The Stockyards Inn serves better whiskey and steak than coffee!" He shook his head to clear the taste.

"Anyway, Cripple is now a war zone. As an officer you would recognize it.

The officer smiled. "A war? In the mountains of Colorado? This is news to me."

"I kid you not, Paul. The parties in conflict are the miners' union and the big owners. No cavalry charges or cannons, but darn near. There are beatings and assassinations. Parts of the camp so tough that the Sheriff is unwilling to go in alone. Neighbors aren't talking. Playground fights at school between children of pro and anti union families. It is not a placid, easygoing place to work and live. There's money to be made, no doubt." He shrugged.

"But I don't like that stuff—like I said, I avoided the army and want nothing to do with gunfire. So rather than get on a mine crew in Cripple, I decided to get out of mining."

Wistfully, he went on. "I love making the earth give up wealth, I really do. But not so much that I want to die for it. What to do next? I grew up around animals. Everyone needs animals, and there won't be a wage squabble between horses and owners. No danger of a strike or muddle of how to handle strikebreakers. So working with our four footed friends seemed like a way to go. I got to talking to folks, and here I am."

He paused, shoving the coffee cup around, unwilling to finish the brew.

"So tell me, why is a purchasing officer for the Royal Army in Colorado? What are you doing here in the old colonies?"

"Colonies? You Yanks kicked us out over a century ago. And now are giving us a run for our money on the world scene. But you ask why am I here?"

He raised his hands, explaining with a flourish.

"The Queen needs horses for her war. Wars. Lots of horses. We have a number of armies in the field. Most of them fighting hot wars, some ongoing low level wars. Nigeria. India. Burma. The Sudan, Egypt, and other spots around the globe. The hot spot right now is South Africa and the damned Boers. For all of that, we want horses and mules. Every soldier at the front requires one or two or more horses and mules to support him. Just how many depends on where and conditions. I am here, Gace, for the Queen's horses."

III

Licia sat ahorse and savored the view from her ranch's high point. Technically it was not her ranch and she wasn't at the true highest place. But there she had the best view, and also the property had been in her family for generations. Her granddad used to kid her that you could see into four states from here. She grinned at the emptiness, no not emptiness but a view full of air, hills, prairie. No buildings, no entrapping trees, just a vista that went on to see forever.

Felicity Heldon—the name on her birth papers—had long looked forward to this. A year ago she had started studies at the New York Institute of Art. Only a few days in she started to dream of her beloved open and unpopulated spaces. Manhattan's Central Park and other riding trails just didn't hold a candle. Even if you took away all the people and let one go in alone, there was no comparison. On many levels the place was a disappointment.

And so were the arts. She fled east, wanting to shed the ranch background and outlook. She had every intention to become part of the arts scene, the New York center of the universe arts scene. Losing those illusions didn't take all that long. That, plus the fact she had to face that she didn't have the talent or drive to make it there. Home now, she had to laugh at her naivete. But the year did teach her something of use: Animals, their welfare, and wide blue skies were in her future.

This was her first full day home. Licia did what she had dreamt of for months: she got out with her horse Sweet Lightning. She—they—ate this up like cream on blueberries, or dewy grass next to a creek. It was exquisite. The wind on her face, the unspoken teamwork between horse and rider, the quiver of joy and excitement from the horse as they galloped. She was reminded again why she loved horses and her ranch. Running free, the climb and the opening vista, no people in sight, it was wonderful. Everything was better than she remembered.

For some reason the sunny morning made her think back to childhood. How she abhorred her given name. Felicity. It was complicated for a kid. Worse, one of her brothers called her 'Cat Town.' That made her cry and she hated him at the time. He could still get under her skin with it. At age three she simply stopped answering to it. Licia she had been ever since.

Coming back to the present, she reined around and headed back to the ranch house. She and her mother were going on a girls' ride. For years they went out together daily, rain shine or snow—only lightning would keep them in. That was one daily ritual she really missed while back east. This would be their first since her return. Licia knew that her mother liked it as much as she did, and both were excited to go.

As the sun climbed to mid morning heights, they met at the corral. The young woman climbed off and led the mare to the stock tank. Her mom's horse was already there. Both drank deeply, enjoying a morning with the return of the long absent daughter. The women remounted and they went past the corral and through the pasture. Passing through a gate they were back into open range. The two rode in companionable, side by side stillness.

The elder broke the silence. "I bet your year in the city felt long. It sure felt like forever for me."

"Well, yeah. I guess in a way it flew. But mostly it drug slow. I felt like I was trying to move a wagon with a seized-up wheel. But it was good for me. I needed the space, the independence, the chance to make my own decisions for good or ill. All in all, it was good."

She smiled at her daughter.

Yes, you seem...happy."

"I have to say that being there on my own sure made me focus and decide on priorities."

"Oh?"

"Yes. I grew up as the ranchers' eldest daughter. For a long time I felt my way was laid out for me. I kind of thought I'd just marry a cowboy and keep the ranch running and the tradition going."

"Oh? You really felt like your life's track was all set?"

"For a long time, yes. But somewhere along the way, as you know I kind of rebelled."

"Kind of? Keeping tabs on you at sixteen was like tracking a wounded bear. And when we caught up you were as ornery as one." She smiled. "But I remembered being sixteen and so did your dad."

Licia smiled too. "I deserved to be locked up in a closet."

"Oh, you'll get yours back some day, don't worry. We're just glad you're home."

Licia mused. "You mentioned sixteen. At that age I suddenly lost interest in barrel racing and in being a hand at branding time. All of a sudden, the arts called to me. I was taken by dance. And painting—oils, watercolor, acrylic, charcoal, you name it, they all spoke to my soul. That's when I set my sights on the East. More than anything, I desired a year in New York City. Immersed in the arts."

She stopped, mother stopped, the horses patient, standing side by side. A spontaneous and awkward saddle bound hug saw the two teeter but stay up.

"And you and dad found a way to let me do it. Thank you."

Licia got back a teary nod. "We were thrilled to see you spread your wings."

It was good to talk, really talk, with her mom. She didn't realize how big a hole in her life she had been ignoring. Licia opened up and went on.

"I have to tell you, it was glamorous and exciting. The full sidewalks, the trolley cars, the vendors, the nonstop hum and dynamic energy, all the things you find in a nonstop city were wonderful and different. That was true at first. But soon enough it palled. Before long it was just crowded dirty and noisy."

She sighed, twice.

"It took me a while to face facts. Life in the west started looking better than it had for years. I wasn't sure" here she nervously glanced over—"I wasn't sure if I wanted to ranch. But I knew I at least wanted something like it: A life in or near the Rockies, out west around animals and clear skies."

A delighted maternal outburst: "If you got that much out of it, the time and money were well spent!"

"Better let me finish before you get carried away with that. I started ditching classes. The art school people were nice enough but had never dirtied a boot or blistered a hand or seen life born and die. They were, are, just too far removed from the life I brought to the city. It was hard to talk with them. So I went out and found a job. I worked training and mending horses at a racing park."

"Oh? I'll bet you met some interesting characters there. And a shady one or two. Did you know I did something like that, and that's where I met your dad?"

"I guess I forgot that. But I didn't meet anyone interesting. Well, yeah, I did. But no one I was remotely interested in romantically. At the track they were real people. I met all sorts of folks, warts and all. And there were some real lulus. My roommates were horrified. Horrified but fascinated, I expect. As for me, I felt at home with the owners, touts, jockeys, stable hands. Even the spectators and bettors."

"Most horse people are good folks."

"Yup. But the horses. Isn't it something how individual they are, how each has unique traits, almost a personality? I loved them and found I loved fighting to have them treated well. And I met others who felt the same. I even met some people trying to grow an organization, a company."

"Oh?"

"Yes. They have an organization to help keep animals from cruelty."

Licia paused, looking around again at the clean open spaces.

"Mother, I have to tell you, it is good to be home. I drew on memories of this kind of scene all winter. Even so, I forgot how much I love this."

A gaze over her and her husband's ranch. "Yes, I understand. I sometimes come here when I have a difficult or discouraging day. This is the place for me to get refreshed. Problems seem to shrink out here, and optimism grows."

Then the gaze fell into her daughter's eyes. "And what do you intend to do now?"

"I guess I had better come clean. Like I said, I didn't attend much of art class after the first few weeks." She glanced over, expecting anger or resentment or rejection.

"Yeah, you mentioned that. So, like I asked, what now?"

"Well. I mentioned that at the track I met folks who are trying to stop animal abuse."

"Oh?"

"And I have a job, mom! I am Western Regional Director for the CPS."

"CPS?"

"Cruelty Prevention Society. We are the voice for the animals being cruelly treated, the advocates for them. Have been since the 1860s. We work with animal owners to help them keep their dumb friends healthy and safe. The whole country west of the Mississippi is mine!"

"Oh? Yours? You going to tell ranchers or stock brokers what to do? That'll go over well coming from a New York based outfit!"

"Yes, mine. I will be working to keep animals safe and well treated. And don't roll your eyes. We don't lecture, we almost never intervene. We do provide help and resources. I suppose if we see a truly cruel act or situation we will try to stop it. But you and I know most ranchers treat their animals and stock well. So do most small owners and most stockyards. But not all people do. And I want to help."

"Well, Felicity, let's talk more about that over coffee back at the house."

She reined her horse around and spurred gently, then hard.

"Race you!"

IV

THE MAN'S BRITISH ACCENT WAS STARTING TO GRATE. GACE'S ears rebelled, not enough to shut it out, but he had to concentrate to get the gist.

"Horses and mules, lots of them, are what we want. Need. As many decent animals as you can round up." Read repeated himself. He waited a moment to be sure he had the floor. "I am one of many officers doing this. We have purchasing operations in most states of the US, in Canada, Argentina, South Africa, and many other locations. We need them by the thousands."

Gace nodded. "I expected as much."

"McNall, it is like this. We—the Royal Army—are working small actions in Africa, India, Malaya, and other of our possessions. The damned natives in all those places, and more, don't want us to stay."

The expression he wore was indignant and incredulous. "The damned fools don't see the value of being in the British Empire."

"Imagine that, people wanting to run their own affairs."

Piers-Read laughed, giving it right back. "Says the man whose government is trying to conquer Cuba and the Philippines."

Gace shrugged and the officer continued.

"Anyway, most places, we have to fight small actions. But as I was saying, in South Africa we're fighting a full scale war. We are fielding regiments, many entire regiments of British and Commonwealth troops. This takes supply and logistics which takes horses and mules. We have to get the supplies and ammunition and medical and veterinary are out to the troops."

He paused, looked around the room. "Our foe, the Boer, lives and fights from his horse. He won't stand and fight like a soldier. Rather he lays in wait and ambushes our men. And he evicts, or worse jails, British citizens in his midst. The Boer runs when outnumbered. We need a full army to catch and subdue him."

"Their strategy sounds good. That's probably what we'd do if someone invaded us."

At that, Piers-Read shrugged but still talked.

"He—the Boer—knows the land like his own farm yard. He doesn't carry a big kit and doesn't keep fixed forts or strongpoints. In fact, his horse is the strongpoint and the kit is just a food bag, blanket and his rifle. This is a new kind of war for us. And their families! They are as feisty as the men! We have had to put them, the women and children, into camp. We gather them so we can feed and shelter them. Concentration camp is what we call it. They are not pretty but are the only way we've found to make them stop fighting us."

The officer was getting worked up. He stopped, calmed himself.

"We need horses to best them. We will mount our infantry and beef up the cavalry. Of course we have artillery which is moved by horse or oxen. And we use mules for our supply trains."

The man paused, thinking or Napoleon's saying that 'an army moves on it's stomach.'

"So that's why the Queen needs lots of horses and mules. Gace, we may have to chase those damned farmers to hell and back. And maybe their families too. And we will pursue them all until we win." Read looked satisfied at his explanations.

He was enjoying talking on Boer tactics and plans, and British counterplans. Meanwhile Gace ran through the names of horse ranchers and wranglers, thinking who would have animals.

"So, Paul, say I have twenty or fifty head and you buy them. What happens then?"

"If it is a lot, hundreds, we'll likely prefer to arrange our own pick up out there. Different for smaller lots like you mention. For them, you or the owner ship them to the stockyards here. We inspect them, take possession, and pay you. Then we gather them in Cheyenne. When we have enough, they go by rail to the coast. Then on a ship to Africa. You don't need to know more than that."

There were some specifications—size, breed, health, and so on. "Like I said, Gace, we inspect each animal. Don't try to send us nags or fourteen year olds. We want fit healthy animals."

"I have some ideas. Will look into it."

Pulling his watch out, the officer checked it then stood and extended his hand.

"Sorry, but I have to go. Meeting with some people. Good talking with you, Gace and I hope we can do business."

The waiter brought a fresh cup of coffee. Gace let it cool and sat, thinking. Trainloads of horses to be sold! He could make a killing.

The wording of that thought gave him a start. Inevitably, he knew, some of the horses going out would not survive A few would not live through the train ride to the coast. And some percentage (no doubt Paul Piers-Read could quote it exactly) wouldn't survive the voyage. And those who survived to land in Africa would be driven to the sound of the guns.

Make a killing. Indeed, he thought. The welfare of those horses was not his business after money changed hands. But still, he felt something ought to be done to give all the horses a decent chance at survival. Someone ought to look out for those animals. He'd heard of some such organization and decided to check them out.

Across town, Cope sat in his room, drapes drawn. The letter was still in hand, but after reading and re-reading, it was limp and ignored. How to make sense of his family's disintegration? He worried at and mulled over what to do. What steps could he take? He had to heal himself, then avenge and act! He pondered how he could move ahead. One step at a time...

Somewhere or sometime during his reporting and investigations he had heard of the CPS. The Cruelty Prevention Society. He thought about his father's, his families' horses and what must be happening to them. The CPS was a uniquely American invention. Who but them would dream up a company to keep animals safe? No one else had ever thought of that! In his reportorial ramblings, he had learned that the CPS now had an office in Denver. It was new and he had made an appointment to visit.

Cope was actually glad it was time to go call on them: action of some sort was better than sitting and wallowing in rage and self pity. He viewed it as an opportunity to get acquainted and make contacts. Looking at the map, it was practically next door, less than twenty blocks. It would be a nice walk.

Eighteen blocks away, a woman looked at a new, small sign. It was freshly affixed to the door. She read it aloud, disbelievingly. 'Cruelty Prevention Society, Western Regional Office.'

She should have been the one to put the sign up! The words, the neat little sign, angered her. After all, she had been working for animals and animal rights in Denver for years. Who were these folks, to drop in from out of town somewhere with their fancy new office?! They should have hired her. She felt insulted and deprived. Her ornery streak was never small, but it got suddenly broader and deeper.

Behind the door sat a young woman, raven haired and sunburnt.

Licia looked at the newcomer, surprised. She was expecting some reporter later but had nothing on the calendar now. What could this gal want. "Can I help you?"

"Who is in charge here?"

"I am. And you are...?"

"Name is Ella. Ella Queue. I have been working animal rights here in Denver for years, maybe decades. Every cowboy and blacksmith in the area knows me and knows I mean business. I make 'em treat animals right. Who are you?"

Licia stood, extended her hand. "I am Licia Heldon, western regional manager of the Cruelty Prevention Society. As you see, we are newly opened here. Welcome! Now, Ella, how can I help you?"

Ella looked at the hand, hesitated as if it was unclean. But she took and shook it vigorously. As she pumped, her voice was almost shrill.

"I care. You know, I stop people in the street if they're beating their horse. Or kicking their dog for that matter. If an animal looks tired or hungry I try to make the owner stop, feed and water the poor dumb thing. Imagine being unable to speak, how helpless. So, Heldon, what do you and your fancy CPS do that I don't? And what gives you the right to come in here?"

"Well, Ella, thank you for your caring and efforts. We at the Cruelty Prevention Society have been looking after animal welfare since the 1860's. It started and its efforts concentrated on where the people and animals are, back east. But the need is everywhere, which is why we opened this office."

Licia wasn't sure this woman was following. She decided to give her credence and calmly went on anyway. "You are right. Animals can't speak up. It is good, Ella, that you try to do it for them. We take a different approach. What we do is try to educate folks so no one, not you or I or anyone else, has to…"

"Educate?! Hell, woman, trying to educate people is a waste of time and energy. People don't want to learn and don't care! You have to grab the halter and stop them! Wrestle the whip out of their hands if need be!" Ella was practically yelling when she finished.

Oh great, Licia thought. How do I get this girl to the loony bin, or at least out of here?"

The door opened and a man walked in with a smile. He glanced at Ella before talking. He had a confident air. The guy had no false bravado, not cocky or intimidating. He was not a big man but somehow filled the room. He appeared fit, strong and confident, but still somehow sad. It was clear that he knew what he was about.

"I'm looking for a Linda or Laura, not sure. Manager of the Cruelty Prevention office."

"You're looking for me. One moment please."

Licia gestured at the unruly woman and walked to the door. She hoped she wouldn't have to take Ella by the elbow and throw her out. But the visitor was docile. Miss Queue had had her say. She looked and felt collapsed, like a rising loaf of bread when a door slams. Ella meekly followed Licia's gesture and went to the exit.

"Ella, we need to talk some more. We have much in common."

Queue meekly nodded, looking at the floor not Licia.

"But I won't have you come in here and yell. Do come back when you have calmed down and we can discuss things. Good bye." Then she did take her visitor by the elbow and nudged her out.

Licia had been standing tense, ready for a confrontation. When the door closed she visibly relaxed.

GACE GRINNED. "LOOKS LIKE I INTERRUPTED SOMETHING."

"Yes, and frankly I'm glad you did. She came out of nowhere and was loudly boasting of her supposed work and efforts. And criticizing mine. No telling how that could have ended."

She extended her hand just like a man would. "I'm Licia Heldon, manager of the Cruelty Prevention Society. Again, thanks. Your timing was exquisite. How can I help you?"

"Gace McNall. Sorry about not remembering your name, Licia. It is nice to meet you." He smiled ruefully. "It wasn't planned—guess it is better to be lucky than good, on the timing."

His rueful smile grew. The grip was firmer than expected. And her hands were calloused like she had handled a rope, or branding iron, or tools, something along those lines. Maybe she wasn't just a soft do-gooding office worker.

She pulled her hand back and waited, looking at him patiently.

"I am a livestock contractor. I buy and sell horses, mules, cattle, sheep, what have you. We're both in the animal business and it looks like you are new in town. So I wanted to stop in, say hello, and get acquainted. With you and your organization."

He paused, then said, "It seems your new office has some competition." The attempt to lighten the conversation didn't cover his unspoken question. Of course that was, 'will you cause me problems?'

She held his gaze a moment longer. He got the impression she was trying to decide, friend or foe?

"Gace, you say? Do you specialize in any way?

V

"Specialize? My specialty is to find owners looking for animals, and animals looking for a new home. And then to match them up. I'm pretty good at it—heck, horses run to me begging to be sold," Gace deadpanned. The words just flowed, and he wondered where on earth they came from.

Licia gaped at the clumsy joke. Then she giggled, and laughed.

"Well, Mr. McNall, it is my pleasure to meet such an extraordinary animal handler. Tell me. Do they come up and nuzzle you or just neigh and scrape their front hooves?"

"Oh, they neigh only when they don't like the buyer's offer. I have made good money by listening to the advice of the neigh-sayers."

She rolled her eyes, stifling another laugh.

"Enough. Seriously. Come, sit. Let me tell you about the CPS. And maybe we can talk more about your business. Perhaps we can help." She motioned to a chair next to her desk as she sat.

"Licia, you say? Unusual but melodic. Is that a nickname?"

"I was christened Felicity, actually Felicity Jane. But didn't like either. Stopped answering to Felicity when I was young. Not sure how Licia came to be used but there you have it. You? Talk about unusual. What is the story with your name, Gace?"

Expected question. He had the story down pat, but today he veered off script a bit.

"Same kind of thing. I got saddled…" at that, he unsuccessfully stopped a smirk, "…with George Armstrong Custer McNall. You know how some parents gave famous namesakes. Mine bought into that effort big time. My brother is Benjamin Franklin and a sister is Clara Barton. Anyway, I didn't like George, found Armstrong peculiar, and no one would let me use 'Cus.' I somehow ended up as Gace."

"Ah." She waited.

"My livestock business. Well, Licia, there really isn't a lot to tell. My efforts are actually simple and straightforward. I match sellers of animals with buyers, buyers with sellers. If it lives in a field or a cage I'll work it. If you need a milk cow or a team of oxen, I'll work it. Once I got a request for a llama as a sheep flock guard. Off beat but I found some and got them set up. Those animals like to live in pairs, not solo. They can be fierce and have been known to trample marauding coyotes, did you know that?"

"No, but somehow I'm not surprised."

"But today, horses are the thing. Horses and mules. Like I say, I'll move sheep or cattle, and even sold a bunch of mink once. Excuse me, I sold a 'company' of mink. That is what a group of those furry biters is called. All well and good, but there is no money there for someone like me. I prefer horses. They are a man's best friend, and a woman's, too. Not dogs."

"Ah."

Gace found her ability to make him talk intriguing. As a boy he hadn't been good at making girls laugh and he did no better with women when he grew older. He was taken with her apparent delight at his quirky humor.

"So if you know anyone looking to buy or sell animals please send them my way. Right now I have a client who wants to buy horses. Horses and mules, by the herd if you got 'em."

Her antenna went up. "Oh? To what end? Who is buying?"

"Well, that is confidential right now. But the buyer is well financed and experienced. Feeding, care and transport of the stock are all well organized and present no problems."

"Ah." She hadn't expected a name, but if they were looking for large numbers and were well financed, they were probably government somehow. Maybe she'd look into that angle. But then again it could be a railroad, or a company opening a new mine, or a racing stable? In any case, she felt it worthwhile to meet a member of the community. She would, she decided, cultivate the contact.

"From time to time I do hear of people looking to buy or sell, but don't get details. We are in the animal welfare end of things. Generally we steer wide of the commercial aspects."

She smiled.

"But I will keep you in mind. That said, remember that we are the Cruelty Prevention Society, not a livestock clearing house. I am first and always concerned about the treatment of the animals. We never want to learn, but all too often do, that animals are not being treated well."

"Yes, I have seen some incredibly skilled and wholesome operations. And some that use their animals as a thing, like they would a wagon or hay rake. It is awful to see and I try to avoid those operations."

She nodded, knowing that all too well.

"To that end, Gace, we will work with anyone to improve the lot of their livestock and other animals. You'd be surprised how some people mistreat even dogs and cats."

He screwed up his courage, not sure why he was doing this so soon.

"Licia, could we maybe talk over dinner? I'd like to learn more about you and the CPS. Would you…"

THE DOOR OPENED ABRUPTLY, FLAPPING OVER AGAINST THE wall with a slam. Licia and Gace stopped talking and looked.

A young man followed the door breathlessly; he was either in a hurry or angry, which was not clear. Something about him immediately stood out. Whatever it was, his dress or posture or how he entered the room? The way he looked at her? Something made her think he was not a native born American.

Before the door swung shut Licia got a glimpse out on the street behind him. On the sidewalk Ella stood waving her arms and talking to someone. The woman was animated and passionate, but the listener did not seem to be paying much attention. Actually it looked like the woman being harangued was trying to get past Ella without being too rude. Good luck, thought Licia. She was glad the crazy woman was occupied and wouldn't try to return to the office.

The newcomer spoke. His English was good and he spoke fluently not haltingly. The trace of accent confirmed her impression of not being native born. Where the accent was from, she couldn't identify.

"I have an appointment with" here he glanced at a piece of note paper, and went on "with a Licia Heldon. Is she in?"

He glanced at Gace. "Excuse me, I don't mean to interrupt."

She glanced at the clock and then her desk calendar. Of course, some reporter had made an appointment to talk with her. It slipped her mind with Gace's coming in.

The man waited a moment then turned to leave. She spoke up.

"That is me, Licia Heldon. Are you Copernicus Oursa? The reporter?"

Cope nodded. "That is me."

"You are right on time. Please give me a moment here."

Turning to Gace, she smiled. "Yes, I would like that." She glanced at the newcomer. "I have a previous commitment here, with a reporter. Good public relations and all. Perhaps you can come back later this afternoon?"

Standing, he grinned. "Of course. At dinner time? Say, six?"

She smiled and nodded. He was happy and floating as he stood and walked past the man, to the door.

Gace and the reporter made eye contact. Gace was ready to smile but there was something about the man...his face was calm. But the eyes were angry, anguished, even desperate. The man was upset about something.

For a moment Gace wondered if he should leave Licia alone. The guy had made an appointment, yes, but anyone could do that. He was a stranger, and possibly volatile. But then, that woman Ella, when he came in, acted unhinged too. He figured this reporter was no threat.

As he went through the door, he turned for another look, just to be sure. The man settled meekly into the chair and pulled out a pencil and notebook. Not a problem, Gace decided. The guy really was a reporter.

"Thank you for taking the time to see me, Mrs. Heldon."

"Happy to do it. I forget, what newspaper is it that you report for?"

VI

Cope set the pad and pencil down. He reached for a business card and handed it to Licia.

She eyed the card as he spoke.

"I work for a newspaper you haven't heard of. It is De Volksstem. It is well established as the voice of the Boer community. We have a reputation for honest reporting and fair treatment. Our home is the city of Pretoria, Africa. Or I should say, it was last I heard."

That struck her as…different. Last he heard? What did that mean?

"Oh?"

He sunk down in the chair, as if pushed and held by a bully.

"I'm sorry. That sounds odd, I know."

She nodded and waited.

"What I mean is things are happening fast in my country. So fast and confusing that it is hard to know what is a fact and what is a partial or entire lie. Right now the British are moving in, invading. We resist but it is very hard. No one knows if or when they will try to put an end to everything they can, everything that gives us strength and tries them. Wherever they are, they try to shut down the life of our people and our communities. Newspapers will be closed or forced to spread British lies."

Licia of course had read of British wars and advances around the world including in southern Africa. That was just newsprint, just a dry story written by some 'objective' reporter. That just meant they hadn't lost a relative and wouldn't get shot and could always go home to the safety of the good old USA. But here was the other side. This person seemed to know the actual effect of cavalry and infantry advancing, destroying as they went. She didn't really didn't know what to say.

"Oh, that must be hard for you."

"Yes. But let's talk about you. My assignment is to learn how you Americans treat and use animals. I imagine that your organization has a part in that story. At least it seems a good place to start learning and telling about it."

Having said his piece, he simply sat back. He didn't look at her for a response. The man just silently looked into the distance, unfocused, almost not even there.

Licia briefly wondered about his vagueness. How unsettling that he was uncertain of his paper's location. Some general statement of his assignment, but no questions for her? Then she saw his discomfort.

"Mr. Oursa. Mr. Oursa, are you alright? Can I get you something, a glass of water perhaps?"

He shook his head as if to chase away a nightmare. He briefly gathered himself, with an effort. Then he looked at her and weakly smiled.

"Yes, I am sorry, it is alright. Tell me what you do here please."

Happy to get started, Licia launched into her spiel.

"Of course animals are important to our every day life and our economy. Most owners treat their animals well. They feed and care for them. Unfortunately not every owner is caring and responsible. The Cruelty Prevention Society has been looking after animals since the 1860s. CPS was formed in New York City after the Civil War. The organization has long been active in the eastern part of the country. This is the first office west of the Mississippi River."

She paused but got no reaction, so continued.

"Our job is simple. We advocate, and sometimes intervene, for animals. Our work is with ranchers, farmers, breeders, stable owners, citizens, companies large and small. CPS will partner with anyone who handles and uses animals. What we do is provide support and information. And we will confront cruelty and mistreatment when and where we find it. In fact, let me find a newspaper article for you…"

The ranch girl and former art student was up on her favorite soapbox, and loving it! Few subjects got her going like animals and the mission of the CPS. As she talked she opened a desk drawer and rooted around for the article. As she pulled it out she looked up and was taken aback.

Her visitor looked intently at the notebook in his lap. His face was wet with tears, silent tears. As she stopped talking, he put hands up over his eyes and choked a sob.

Should she be afraid or concerned? Was the man mad or somehow overcome? She glanced at the door, judging whether she could get to it before he could. He seemed calm and sad, not angry or deranged. Taking a chance, she let compassion win out.

"Sir? Mr. Oursa! What is wrong? Can I help you?" She took a cloth from another drawer, got up and warily approached around the desk. "Here, this may help. Let me get you a drink of water."

He wiped his eyes with the handkerchief. "I am sorry, Mrs. Heldon. Forgive me. I just received some bad news. I try to push it away and do my job, but it comes back, it won't leave me alone. Try as I might, it overcomes me even as I try and fight it."

He looked bleakly at her. "You see, your voice reminds me of my sister's. When I closed my eyes it is as if she is telling me about animals. She is kind and compassionate too. Hearing her—you—reminds me of the bad news. And that took me over the edge."

Sipping the glass of water she offered, he was able to collect himself. 'Over the edge.' Just what did that mean, she wondered.

"Do you want to talk about it? Getting it out may help. Tell me about your sister."

He again choked a sob. "It is safe here in America. I am drawing a big salary for a fat and easy reporter's job. No offense, but I shouldn't be talking to attractive American women about trivial things. Well, animal treatment isn't trivial but it is not serious, not life and death."

"Ah." She nodded, unsure what he really meant.

"I am a Boer who is too far from home."

Ah, she realized. He was far from the war consuming his country. He went on.

"My family, my people, are in southern Africa. Where we have been for centuries. They are fighting the British, the Engelse. And they are dying. Too many Boers are dying but not enough Engelse."

That explained his accent, she thought. He was still speaking.

"I just received mail, a letter. I don't know how it got out past the British or even when it was written. Who knows when these things happened. But I know that my father is killed, the farm he built from nothing is destroyed—burnt by the damned British."

"Oh, Mr. Oursa. I am so sorry."

"A troop of horsemen came out of nowhere and did it. Then they gathered my sister, my mother, my brothers. They were rounded up like stray cattle, they had nothing. And then they were herded, made to walk, to a concentration camp. A concentration camp! Our neighbors probably are there too, I do not know for sure. Those damned English are scorching the earth, burning and killing everything!"

His anguished voice was sharp as obsidian.

"I feel a helpless fool: Here I am asking you about animals while my people suffer. And I can do nothing, nothing about it!"

Momentarily without words, she gathered herself. "Oh Mr. Oursa. That is awful. I can't imagine—I feel helpless myself. How can I help you?"

Drying tears on his face, he stared dully at the floor.

"I have to avenge this. Somehow I have to make those damned British pay." This he said in a monotone and she had to strain to hear it.

Her mind flying, one phrase came to mind. "I want to know more about this 'concentration camp' you spoke of."

Cope made to stand but then remained sitting. "The damned Engelse are gathering, herding, forcing the Boers into fenced jails. They are nothing but open air prison camps! For Boer families, and others too, who have done nothing to the damned invaders! Having people in prison, feeding them just enough to stay alive, makes it easier for the Engelse to watch and control."

He shook himself. It reminded her of a dog shaking after a swim, making ready to face the world.

"Thank you for your time, Mrs. Heldon. I am sorry but I must go. And you will hear more about these camps, much more. My newspaper will shout British atrocities to the world. I will come another time to learn about you and your CPS. Thank you."

He stalked out, brushing shoulders with a man coming in. They exchanged glances but didn't speak.

The new visitor stood ramrod straight. The man was dressed as if for a formal Tea in a wool three piece suit. He was in early middle age, had a sunburned outdoor complexion and a hawk nose. His tie was tightly knotted and straight. She got the impression it wouldn't dare flap or otherwise be out of position.

The newcomer glanced around the room as if taking inventory before spoke.

VII

The newcomer's British accent was unexpected. It sounded oddly out of place, coming just after Cope's anguished, European like accent. The words were delivered somehow luxuriantly but were also loud. Licia couldn't decide if it was tinged by arrogance or cockiness, not that there was much difference between the two.

"My name is Paul Piers-Read." He stopped, awaiting acknowledgment.

Licia sat back down at her desk and looked him over, letting him wait half a beat.

"Yes, Mister Read. Nice to meet you. How can I help you?"

"It is Piers-Read, not Read. Piers-Read." The tone of this was headmaster to student. He paused to be sure she got the point.

"This is the office of the Cruelty Prevention Society is it not?"

"Yes it is. I am Licia Heldon, manager. Have a seat, make yourself comfortable, please." She gestured at the chair next to her desk. "How can I help you?"

He produced a card. "I am the officer in charge of a purchasing mission here in the Rocky Mountains. We are looking to buy horses and mules."

She glanced at the card, set it carefully down, face up. "British Royal Army, working for the Queen Empress, Victoria. I have to say that you are a long way from home."

"Yes, well, London is a week or two away, I agree."

"Tell me, Mr. Piers-Read, don't you have horses at home and throughout your Empire?

Licia almost repeated the 'Mr. Read' just to jab a hole in his stuffed shirt, but restrained herself.

"Of course. But the Royal Army has interests and operations all around the globe, Mrs. Heldon. Among them India, Burma, Egypt, West Africa, South Africa, Rhodesia, plus supporting our friends in Canada, Australia, New Zealand, and there are others."

He pulled out a pipe and pouch. "May I?"

"By all means." Actually she abhorred smoking, especially pipes and cigars. But she was curious where this was leading and figured if he was comfortable he would keep talking. He took a minute or two, like pipe users everywhere, to load, tamp, light, and draw the smoke. Soon the room smelled and looked murky. But for the lack of noise they could have been sitting inside a steel mill.

He cleared his throat. "An operation, wherever located, creates needs and demands. We must move our troops, armaments and supplies. Evacuate and care for the sick and wounded. And keep tabs on the opponent at hand. We have found, over the years, best ways of doing this. Often, almost always, it is better to buy animals where we can. It is not always more convenient, I'll give you that. But that way we are certain of number and quality. If we buy locally sometimes we take so many animals that the local farmers can't find any to help them work. That drives the men and their families to the opposition which is the last thing we want. Plus, like I say, we want to have our pick of quality. Another factor which isn't convenient is, the animals then need to be moved to where they are needed."

He stopped to fuss with his pipe, apparently paying it attention but actually deciding what to say next.

"Fortunately the British merchant fleet is huge and is up to the task. Our demands are a drop in the bucket compared to other shipping around the Empire."

He paused, gazed almost affectionately at his pipe. "The animals we acquire are used for such purposes as we decide. Mounted troops, supply, and moving artillery are the main things."

She picked up his card, looked closer at it, again set it down. "Should I call you mister or Major?"

He laughed. "I wonder that sometimes, too. I am an active duty officer. But right now I am detailed to work with civilians and commercial operations, in the civilian world. I will put my uniform back on and go back to being a Major, an officer in the field, somewhere down the road. Yes, please, call me Mister, Mrs. Heldon."

"Alright, Mister Piers-Read. Thank you for clarifying what you are looking for and why. That is good to know."

He nodded, smiled.

"Up front I want to be clear that we do not buy, trade, or sell animals. The Cruelty Prevention Society is not a commercial operation in any way. CPS's purpose, or as you military types put it, our mission, is to educate owners and support good treatment of animals. If need be, we will step in and try to stop flagrantly cruel treatment. Often, we have found, such unkindness stems from ignorance not malicious intent. So the education part is important."

"Quite." His pipe was cool and he found a wastebasket to empty it into, which took a few moments. Licia hoped the embers were out.

As the charred tobacco fell into the bin, he continued.

"Well, my purpose today is simply to introduce myself and get acquainted. No doubt you will hear more of me and my mission. I just wanted you to have a face to put with the name on the card." He smiled as if to imprint a friendly image in her.

"Feel free to contact me at any time with questions or concerns. And I want to emphasize to you that we know animals. We handle thousands of animals all over the world. We know how to feed and care for them, transport them, and heal them if need be. The Royal Army have done so for hundreds of years. We have much common ground when it comes to handling and care of animals, and their humane treatment."

She nodded. "I imagine you have literally written the book on animal handling. So, Paul, tell me about your dealings. I imagine you wheel and deal and find horses or mules you like and strike a bargain. What happens after you hand over the money? Where are you buying?"

He chuckled. "We buy wherever there are animals, which is to say, everywhere. What happens in the course of business? We take them over and check each animal thoroughly for health. We of course look before we buy and will reject sick or weak ones. But we want only strong healthy specimens. If at first they need something minor we take care of it—new shoes or what have you. Then we send them on."

"Send them on from a holding pen? A rented ranch? Where are the horses and mules taken? How? The Royal Army certainly isn't using them here."

He smiled, not amused. "No, we got our walking papers from you Yankees over a hundred years ago." He waited until she nodded acknowledgment.

"The current batch we're buying are headed to Africa. Capetown, to be exact." He realized he probably shouldn't have said that, but it wasn't exactly a secret. The newspapers were saying the same things. "The Boers are acting up and there are new mines to be protected. We—our men there—get around and get control of the crazy Dutch farmers by riding horses and mules."

He paused, grinned. "I think you get my drift. Anyhow, the animals will be sent by rail to a port, and then by ship. Of course, what we do with our fairly bought property is no concern of yours."

"Oh, they go by rail and ship. What are your guidelines for number of animals per shipping compartment? How many are you buying? Perhaps we could inspect your facilities and review your practices?"

The man reddened and was ready to launch at her. But he remembered although he was an officer she was not a private. No one out in the civilian world had to jump to his command. He smoothed and tamped his temper and smiled icily.

"The specific numbers are not your concern. In fact it is a most secret matter and I can't talk about it. Again, know that the Crown's Royal Army has been raising, using and caring for animals for hundreds of years. We successfully utilize and take care of them in an unimaginable variety of climate and terrain. We needn't hear from a new group of 'advisors' with limited experience."

He stood and nodded. "Thank you for your time, Mrs. Heldon. I'll let myself out."

Licia sat quietly, thinking. She came back west to come home and also to help and protect animals. But she was finding herself, possibly, in the midst of a tussle. Just today. Two men wanted to buy or sell horses and another's life was torn up by the users of some of those horses. She had a unique seat at the circus. None of them knew what she knew.

She sighed. The animal welfare business looked to get real interesting. If not for dinner with Gace, she would go out to the ranch and ride her horse. There was nothing that equine therapy couldn't solve.

VIII

Licia perused the menu, weighing which item looked most tasty and interesting. She felt a little surprised: Enjoying a glass of wine in a nice restaurant was almost as relaxing as riding across a meadow. At least for tonight that was so. The Rocky Mountain Trout looked pretty good; she would order that. She watched as Gace perused the menu.

"Tell me about your day, Gace."

"It was good. I stopped in to introduce myself to an industry contact. She swept me away—off my feet, not into the trash bin, praise be. And here we are. Best cold call I've made in years!"

She rolled her eyes and halfway stifled a smile. "Besides that."

"Typical day, talk talk with folks. Didn't get to see even one horse or mule today, at least none for sale. One thing, I did meet an Army officer looking for horses. Actually several of them. Both on buying binges of one kind or another. And so far what I've been able to find, checks out."

"Oh? Tell me."

"The first was a Captain in the US Army. Cavalry officer and I bet he'd rather be back in the field with his horses and troops, not here. Tells me they are happy to take wild ones.

Would prefer, I understand, to break and train them. Not have to undo civilian training first. That part of things thing is kind of outside my area."

"Oh? Wild horses? How do they get rounded up?"

"I don't know for sure, Licia. I could barely understand his Texas twang. We left it that I didn't have wild animal availability right now but would call if I found I could help him."

He chose a meal and closed his menu. "But I hear there are big roundups in northwest Colorado and also in Wyoming. Lots of horses up there."

"The guy was from Texas, huh? Y'all and all?"

"Yup, and dressed as a civilian horseman, big belt buckle, Stetson and all. But the way he asked questions and answered mine tell me he knows horses. I imagine he'd be entertaining over a beer sometime, but doubt that'll happen."

He paused. "And the second army guy was different as night and day."

Licia had a feeling she knew what was coming.

"Oh?"

"He was—is—a Brit. Officer, gentleman, heigh ho and all. He didn't seem to have a lot of horse knowledge, in terms of personally caring for them. He has ridden but isn't a horseman, know what I mean? But he sure knows what he and his Royal Army are looking for. All about numbers and types of horses and mules. A British soldier—even in civilian clothes—is the last person I expected to deal with."

She nodded. "I know the type. The reason I ask is an Englishman came by the office, not long after you left. He came in just as the guy who came in, the reporter, left. I'd bet a month's wages it was the same man."

"Paul Piers-Read is who I met. Is that your guy too?"

She laughed. "Yes. Not Mister Read, I'll have you know. Mister Piers-Read. And I agree, he gave me chapter and verse on how the British use horses and mules all around the globe."

"Must be his sales spiel. I got a lecture too."

"Well, I was sure impressed." She rolled her eyes in denial of that.

"Today was not typical. Usually I have the office quiet and to myself. Today it rained men in there! After you things happened fast and are kind of complicated. Come to think of it, it started with that Ella Queue woman before you came in. What a piece of work she is. I don't know where to begin!"

"Try me. Complicated is alright. Tell me, did you hear the one about an Englishman, a do gooder, an ex-miner and a reporter?"

She smiled. "I'm not good at improvising. But there is a story or two here, let me get it out as I can." Pausing, she shook her head as if to clear it.

"First the reporter. Odd name he has: Copernicus, Copernicus Oursa. Goes by Cope. His job was supposedly to find out and report on what the CPS does. And also write on how we Americans handle animals. We made small talk for a minute or two. He asked a few questions around CPS and animals. Boiler plate stuff, nothing insightful or hostile. Then he broke down."

"Broke down? What do you mean?"

"He was distant, then suddenly he started crying and sobbing. I wasn't sure whether he was a mad man or a wretch. It was the latter, thank God. My voice apparently reminded him of his sister. It turns out he works for some African newspaper...."

"Odd, he didn't look African."

"Not funny, Gace. He is a Boer. Boers are settlers of European stock who have lived in southern Africa for centuries. They're ornery and independent, have been left alone for a long time. Independent farmers and small merchants, not an urban society. But now gold and diamonds were found on their territory. That put them in the crosshairs. The Brits are trying to turn them out or at least tame them."

"Ah yes, the love of money and all…"

She shrugged. "He, Cope just today I guess, got word his father was killed by British troops in the war there. And the family farm was burnt and his family—mother and siblings—taken to a camp. He doesn't know if they are safe or even alive. The poor man was alternately angry then in tears."

"Oh. That is not good. I feel bad for him and those Boers. Hard to give up their independence and the run of the place. But it sounds like they're starting to feel the British heel on their necks. Not something I'd wish on my worst enemy."

"That is where the visiting Englishman comes in. So to speak."

The food was delivered and talk lagged.

"Mmm, this trout is good. How is your meal, Gace?"

"It is seasoned and done just right, and is hot. Almost as good as the company tonight! You were saying Englishman?"

"Ah yes, the Englishman. What did Cope call them? Engelse. That is apparently the Boer word for them. So, our Engelse officer walked in just as Cope got himself together and left. The poor guy was too upset to talk CPS or animals. But before he left, he did swear vengeance for his family. And he said he'd be back."

She smiled, reached over and patted his hand. "The office had a revolving door today. Before you came in I had a visit from a woman convinced she should have my job. Name Ella, Ella Queue. I'm not sure she is all there."

He smiled. "She did seem addled. I'm glad I came in when I did. She seemed about ready to throw a chair."

She continued. "Then Cope came in and you left. Like I said, he started the interview then froze up and fell apart sobbing. His story came out and he vowed he'd get even with the invaders. Then he left, but rubbed shoulders with the Englishman who came in. They didn't talk and it is a good thing. But I repeat myself, sorry."

The waiter came by. "How were the meals? Will you want dessert?"

Licia glanced at him. "Just coffee for me please."

Gace nodded. "The same."

For a moment the talk centered on their meals, then went back to the day's goings on.

"So the Englishman and Boer didn't talk, which like you say probably prevented a scene."

"Yup. No talk. Cope was out the door and on a mission to tell the world about the war. Or maybe do something, who knows. And like you found out, the Brit wanted to talk about it too."

"Why would he tell an animal rights office about that?"

"He said he wanted to get acquainted. My bet is he was trying to stop us from causing him problems. He doesn't want us looking around their operations, I'll tell you that. He all but sneered at CPS as a new group which knows nothing about animals compared to to the Royal Army. I intend to keep an eye on him and his efforts at buying horses."

Licia was intent on the comings and goings of the day. She suddenly wondered what Gace thought of the Royal Army and its purchasing mission.

"Sorry, I was so taken by Cope's misery I didn't think about you and the Royal Army. Are you going to do business with them?"

"Yes, I think I will look into it. Their checks won't bounce and they do know how to care for and safely use animals. I will be able to move several large herds, none of this one horse at a time rigamarole. It should be good, if he and his 'mission' check out like I think they will."

She nodded and he went on.

"So, what is this about this Cope's family being sent to a camp?

"I asked the same thing but couldn't get much out of him. Some sort of open air prison or jail. I suspect there will be something in the newspaper about it soon."

He stood and offered his arm. "Want to walk a little?"

IX

As Licia stood to take his arm and stroll, Gace thought back to his meeting with the British purchasing officer. One of the last things he said was, "If you get me a look at good horses, I'm ready to write a check."

"You know, Licia, I really do think I may sell some horses and mules to Mister Piers-Read."

"Oh? If you get anywhere tell me about it. I am dying to see how they handle animals. I know they use horses and mules routinely. But I'm curious how they handle herds of new animals in transit Can't imagine their methods are inhumane. But they are about winning wars, not animal welfare."

"I always watch how potential buyers treat their stock. If I see cruelty or hunger—or just plain stupidity—I don't deal. These limeys may be big and rich but I'll watch them the same as I would a local farmer. Yes, I'll keep an eye on their methods and let you know. We may have to talk on it over dinner again sometime."

Before she could respond, he deadpanned, "But I really do think it is time to rustle up some horses."

"Not funny mister. If you say that out in the field, you'd likely have to do some fast talking to the local Sheriff. Or worse."

She stopped, turned, so they were looking at each other. "And thanks, I'd like to learn more about the Royal Army horses over dinner some time."

"Let's plan on it. I should probably walk you home and call it a night. I have a pretty big day tomorrow."

MANY COMPETITORS OF HIS WENT WEST, TO THE MOUNTAIN ranches. Gace tried to work smart, and figured there was a better way. He had little interest in spending time fending off competitors. The trick was to go where there were few competitors, allowing him to build relationships. Seeing and selling herds would follow easily from that.

The next morning saw him on the train headed east, to Colorado's 'other' farm and ranch region. His research had shown that the eastern half of the state accounted for the lion's share of agricultural income. It suited him that few of his peers went out on the plains under its big skies.

The strategy would pay off. Horsemen and cattle ranchers were happy to see him. Pickings were abundant and he had the arena pretty much to himself.

Today he was going to Byers, a town about fifty miles from the statue at Colfax and Broadway. The statue there was the traditional measuring point. Near the capitol building, it was the terminal of the trails to the Colorado goldfields in the '50s and '60s. Distances to wherever started there.

There were a number of towns out east, large and small. Many had been built by the railroads. The rail managers knew how far a train could go before it needed to have its boilers refilled. Towns were laid out, more or less evenly spaced, to be a watering point for the engines. Over time many of them languished. Byers was one that grew and thrived. The settlement sat along Bijou Creek. The Bijou—French for jewel—drained much of east central Colorado, flowing north into the South Platte.

The town became and remained an important stop. No longer just a water tower with a saloon nearby, it had added to itself. Byers was the area's trade center. Stockmen and farmers from miles around did business there. Merchants, saloonkeepers, and hotel owners set up shop. The ag men met, swapped, gossiped and socialized there, as did their families and hired hands.

The train pulled in on time. Gace had telegraphed ahead and was expecting to be met.

A young man stood on the platform, eying each person who got off. He was twenty years old, give or take. He stepped forward.

"Mr. McNall? I'm Ted Moore. Mr. Owens asked me to meet you. How was the trip? Do you have any bags? I will be showing you around today. If you have any questions, please ask away."

"No, it is just me, no bags. And call me Gace, please. None of this Mister McNall business."

Moore walked to a carriage. "Alright, Gace. Right now you and I will take this to the ranch. Out south. The drive will take half an hour or forty minutes. The train ride from Denver is getting shorter and faster these days, isn't it? The railroad is getting better, faster equipment. At least it looks like that to me."

"Yes, we're seeing new equipment and new lines. I understand David Moffat, the banker, is getting back in the railroad game. Word is, he is planning to build a line through the mountains to northwest Colorado. And on to Salt Lake City."

Ted smiled. "Yes, my girl out at the ranch was telling me about that. She works in the kitchen and her parents have a place near Boulder. I hope to go see it some time. Anyway, she tells me that the road, Moffat's road, will be near there. It will go along Eldorado Mountain and then up South Boulder Creek. That will be a real good deal when it is done. She tells me her folks and brother expect to profit from that project. Odessa is excited about new jobs and opportunities. Things ought to open up for for them and their neighbors, and the whole area."

He was quiet for a moment, a smile on his face. Gace figured he was thinking about his Odessa, not Moffat's railroad. Turning a corner out of town, he came back to business.

"So, Gace, I understand you are interested in horses?"

"I deal in all kinds of livestock, Ted. Cattle, sheep, I did one poultry deal, and yes, horses. And mules. Have to say I like the horses best."

"Well, this is the place. We raise horses and sheep. A few cattle, but mostly for our own use. This is good horse country."

He looked from Gace to the horizon.

"It goes on forever, the land and the view. Mr. Owens has been here for twenty or more years. He had a tavern in town but sold it for the ranch. He jokes that sheep are easier to manage than drunk cowboys! He has hundreds of acres, not sure just how many. A lot, to be sure. Mr. Owens does know his business. You want horses, we have horses."

Gace looked around. The plains were flat but not really. They undulated and seemed endless, like the ocean. Not that Gace knew the sea, but he imagined what it must be like. There were mountains to the west and only sky to the south, north and east. In the distance he saw the coal smoke exhaust from the steam locomotive as it moved away. Otherwise the view was deep blue over green. The blue overhead had a few puffy clouds. The fields at eye level looked lush and green at this season. Grazing livestock dotted the land as far as he could see.

"This does seem like good horse country."

Ted nodded. "It is that. There is room, plenty of it, for grazing, enough water, and winters aren't too harsh. Oh, we get a blizzard or two every year. The sheep tend to drift with the wind and can get stuck at a fence. Stupid animals just stand there and suffocate in the drifts. Cattle have been known to do that too. So we need to drive them in if we see a blizzard coming. The horses and mules take care of themselves. They'll do just fine thank you very much. Anyway, you are right. This is fine country."

He swept a hand around. "I am repeating and repeating, but sometimes I just can't help myself. It goes on forever, doesn't it? You can see clear into tomorrow, the air is so pure and open and clean!"

A few miles south of town they came towards a substantial house with barn and corrals. Ted pulled up and a man came to take the team and carriage.

"We'll ride out from here but first let's you meet the man. Come on into the house."

A fiftyish man with piercing eyes and a goatee stood from a paper strewn desk.

"Mr. McNall? I'm Charles Owens." His Irish lilt caught Gace off guard. He nodded to a woman sitting across the room. "This is my farm manager, Mrs. Moore."

A woman of the same age stood and offered her hand. "Nice to meet you." Her Irish accent was barely noticeable. It had been sandpapered down through time and use. Gace supposed she had been here for years, speaking thinking and hearing the American version of English.

Owens sat and made small talk. "McNall, you come well recommended. Several ranches in the area have done business with you, I understand.

Gace nodded. "Yes, I am an admirer of Byers bred stock."

Owens smiled. "So you are looking to buy horses and mules. Those, we have. But before Ted takes you out to look some over, I am curious. Who is your buyer?"

Gace smiled. "Well, lots of folks want horses. I will work with most anyone." He paused.

Owens nodded, waiting.

"Not trying to avoid the question, Mr. Owens. It is just that I am a free agent; I work for no one. Rather I bring buyers and seller together. Right now, I have a large well funded group looking for horses and mules."

Owens and the elder Moore exchanged glances. Gace was curious what had gone between them.

"Oh, so large and well funded. How large and how deep are their pockets? Just who might that be?"

X

Gace was drinking in wide vistas and horse trading out in Byers. He truly enjoyed this give and take, and really liked getting out of town to real life.

Back in Denver, Cope was not having a wide open, enjoyable day. Truth be known, he was having trouble focusing. His assignment on paper was to be a journalist. Travel America and learn about animal treatment and the livestock industry. All well and good. But he also had other duties.

Cope thought back to his last meeting with his boss, the editor. The man gave him his written instructions about the animals. He sat back and gazed at Cope long enough to make him uncomfortable, then spoke.

"There's more, Oursa. This is for your ears only, and I won't write it down. You are to take pulse of American public opinion. On the War. The 'Boer War' as the Engelse call it. Their invasion of our homeland. We don't want you to speak out on it—don't get into arguments. Just listen and observe. And tell us. File that information separately from the animal stories. Any questions?"

"Can I take action if I see some way to help our cause?"

"No. You are not a spy nor an agent. You are to collect information, from public and freely available sources only.

We do not want you to do anything which would cause trouble or bring attention to you. Is that clear?"

"Yes. Talk to people, gather information, report. No heroic work."

"Good. Go, and good luck, Cope."

Cope took ship and came to the US, ending up in Denver. It had been alright, talking with stable owners, veterinarians, blacksmiths, and the like. Even that railroad man in downtown Denver.

Then the letter.

He had been blue, dazed, in a fog in the days since he learned of his family's troubles. And he still felt silly about making a fool of himself crying in front of that woman. Today he sat and stewed. Cope knew he had to get out of the rut. He had to do something, even knowing there was no way to help his mother and siblings. He just hoped they were still alive and healthy. There had to be a way to find that out...

Determination grew. Alright, so he couldn't help them directly. He could do his job, at least enough to keep food on the table. But to heck with the editor. He was at a desk thousands of miles away. Easy for him to say Cope shouldn't act or do anything to help the Boer cause. Well, he would do everything he could. Any way he could find to hurt the Engelse or help the Boers, he would do. Some of it he would have to do on the sly, or under another name. But do it he would.

So, he'd file stories and keep his editor happy. But most of his time and energy would go to try and help his Boer people. And go against the British. He would do whatever he could.

He realized his reporter's credentials were valuable. A tool to help him uncover and gather information was powerful.

He had the beginnings of a plan. He wrote a cousin living in New Orleans and telegraphed his boss.

> Dear Cousin,
>
> You have heard of the death of my father, on Commando? I received word of this just a few days ago and am not sure just when it happened. Tell me, how is your family faring over there?
>
> I am working here in the US as a reporter. My paper is in De Volksstem out of Pretoria. Or at least Pretoria was the base when I left. Not sure now due to the Engelse invasion. I am still filing stories and being paid, I can tell you that! Along those lines, I need your help to do my job and to help all the Boer families which have been harmed. Please give me contacts you have with Boer folk or sympathizers here in the US (or Canada, Mexico etc).
>
> Pray for my mother and siblings who are in a camp—not sure if that is better or worse than to be with my father. I pray yours are safe and well. Write me.
>
> Cope

The telegram was of course shorter and abbreviated.

> Intend to slow focus on animal stories comma report more on B activities here and atrocities there stop Advise status Pretoria office stop Advise any US based Boer friends stop. Oursa

He sat looking out the window. Who else could he call on? Idly he thumbed through the Rocky Mountain News. There was a man who looked familiar. Pondering, he remembered, it was the man who came in to the Cruelty Society office as he left.

Cope scanned then carefully read the story. Anger grew with every sentence. He was a British officer buying horses?! Damn, the guy was helping those Engelse kill men like his father and burn farms! He had to find out about this man, to fight and stop him. Before he knew it, he was up and out the door, paper in hand.

Licia looked up at the door's opening.

"Mrs. Heldon. Do you have a moment?"

It took a moment then she remembered, it was the Boer. Named Orr or something unusual like that. Oursa, that was it! He carried a newspaper and seemed to have his emotions under control. That was a relief.

"Yes, Mr. Oursa, come in. I hope you are feeling better today."

"My apologies for making a scene. It was distressing."

"It wasn't much of a scene. And you had good reason to feel badly. Come in and sit, please." She smiled and closed a file. "I was reading a boring report which can wait."

He slapped the newspaper on her desk, folded to the picture and article about the purchasing mission. "This man, this Major Piers-Read." Accusingly he hissed, "He was here."

"Yes, he was. Why?"

"He is buying horses for the Royal Army." His tone remained accusatory, almost shrill. Licia wondered if she was wrong in thinking he was under control.

"Yes, that is my understanding."

"He is looking for horses to be ridden by the men who killed my father and others!"

"I'm afraid that is so, Mr. Oursa. The horses he buys here, at least some of them, will end up in Africa and be used by Royal Army troops."

Cope nodded. "I almost, accidentally, knocked him down as I left. If I'd known who he was, I would have."

"I am sorry this distresses you. The man dropped in, unannounced. He stopped in to advise what he would be doing. Just a courtesy call is all. He didn't ask for anything. Nor did he give much information, really."

"I need to find him. Where is he?"

"Well now, sir, that is not for me to say." She fixed him with a firm look, not quite a stare. He did not shrink, rather returned the look. She continued.

"Where he is today, right now, I couldn't—and wouldn't—tell you even if I knew. His whereabouts and doings are not your or my business. Nor would I tell him of your business if he asked."

Cope stiffened at that, leaned forward as if to follow up on it.

Licia smiled calmly. "No, he did not ask about you. Far as I know, from his statements and his reaction to brushing by you, is that he does not know you. Or even know about you."

Cope stared. "These men are killing my people. I will do anything I can think of…"

She fixed him again with the direct look.

"I mean, I will do anything I can within the law to thwart them." There, it was out. He felt better saying it.

Licia felt bad for this man who was far from home and had very bad news of his family. On top of the fact that his people were being invaded and abused. A thought occurred.

"Well, as a reporter, I would think that your readers will want to know about him and his efforts. And what he and his Royal Army intend to do with the horses they buy."

She consulted a city directory, found a page, turned it around for him to see. She pointed at an address which he memorized.

"This is public information. If you happen to be in the area you might find it of interest to stop in and talk. Let me know how it goes."

"Thank you, Mrs. Heldon."

"Call me Licia. Just so you know, I am not married. And I wish you good luck with Piers-Read."

Cope all but sprinted out to go for the Royal Army's office. On the street he stopped and thought where and how to get there. It was located out at the stockyards, not downtown near where he was. He shrugged. Going out there was something of a jaunt, not a two block walk. Better go home and prepare.

As he arrived a delivery boy was knocking on his door.

"Can I help you?"

"Are you Mr. Oursa?"

Cope nodded.

"Yes? Good! Telegram for you! Two of them!" He held them out with one hand, the other extended hopefully. Cope dropped in a penny for each.

"Thanks, Mister!" And he was gone.

One was from New York, the other New Orleans. New Orleans first. He started to open it but waited until inside to read.

XI

Holding the 'grams, he carefully stepped in. Both were begging to be read and he made it fast. First, the new Orleans message from his cousin.

He knew he'd have to skim then re- and re-re-read. Telegrams weren't cheap—you paid by the word. So they were always short, even curt. The full message was literally to be had only by reading between the lines. And often by mulling them over and coming back an hour later.

Of course he hoped but doubted that his cousin had better news from home than he had:

> Condolences yr father prayers the family stop Last heard my father went on commando stop Mother and sister left farm driving cattle and wagonful supplies before Engelse torched house stop No further word stop Contact Boer general Samuel Pearson stop See Bill Haywood at west fed miners union Denver stop God Bless stop

His editor was a little more cryptic.

> Approve focus on war first animals next stop. Royal Army buying horses mules US stop. Pretoria office occupied stop Continue to send stories here stop Gd luck stop

---

COPE SAT. HE LOOKED FROM ONE TELEGRAM TO THE OTHER, thinking.

First, of course, he thought about the goings on at home and with his cousin:

So his uncle went out on commando like his brother—Cope's father—had. He fretfully hoped his uncle hadn't been killed too. Commandos were common knowledge among Cope and his Boer peers. Now the journalist turned activist intended to make sure the world knew about the commando.

The commando, he remembered fondly, fearfully and respectfully, was a working get-together. It was a group of Boer horsemen/farmers who met, carrying arms, wearing work clothes. He remembered his father and others in a slouch hat and dun colored trousers and coat. With a week or two's food rolled in a blanket tied behind their saddle, they went on the offense. They were defending their homes, looking for British, Engelse, to harass and kill. They would be out on the hunt until they ran out of ammunition and food, usually days or weeks.

At first the women and children were left behind, safe at home and unharmed. As the British offense unfolded, that security evaporated. Increasingly they were molested, run off, even killed. Even so, the families left behind were self sufficient, adaptable folks. As his aunt had shown! She too had supplies, shelter, and no doubt a shotgun which she knew how to use. But she had to leave the homestead. As she fled, her aim was to avoid, not confront, the Engelse. Cope surely hoped she could stay on the move, stay relatively safe. That she didn't end up in a concentration camp like his mother. He closed his eyes and wished her Godspeed.

After a moment, he considered his cousin's recommendation of Samuel Pearson. There were more questions than answers.

A Boer general? Here in the US? How could that be? Why was he here, not at the front in southern Africa, and what was he doing in America? More importantly, how could he help? Why go to see Bill Haywood at the Western Federation of Miners? Of course. Haywood would have a way to contact Pearson. Did Pearson want to be contacted and would he reply, was the question.

Cope pondered then set the telegram aside. He'd go see this Haywood character soon.

Next step was to look and understand what his editor was really saying:

So his boss agreed Cope should focus on the war then animals. He was glad to hear the editor saw it was time turn over rocks. Time to expose the British and their dirty little war. Or at least do the best we can to get the word out.

He sat, thinking, and literally scratched his head. How about the Royal Army buying horses left and right? How did that fit in with his stories about British atrocities? One thing was sure, he was glad to be given free rein. Couldn't wait to expose the Big British Empire for their brutality and crimes! At least that is how he chose to take it. He would send stories to New York alright, and try to get them local and regional exposure too.

He made a mental note to see if that Cruelty woman—which bizarrely brought an image of her in a short black robe sulkily swinging a whip in slow circles above her head. He banished that vision before it took him in. He wanted to see Licia to learn if she had any contacts with local papers, nothing more. Maybe he could get articles in some of them, he hoped. The wider he cast the word about the Engelse, the better.

Cope stood and stretched, deciding it was a good time to go and see this Bill Haywood person. He looked in the city directory. Finding the address of union, he got a drink of water then started walking. It wasn't far, only fifteen or twenty blocks.

"How can I help you?" The secretary looked like a boxer, one who had stepped into the ring many times. His coat was no doubt a large, but it wouldn't button over his big chest. The tie, a nice wide fabric one, looked tiny. The man glowered, a natural born gate keeper, big and strong with a crooked nose. He looked the unannounced visitor up and down, trying to put him in his place. And not too subtly checking him for trouble, a knife or a gun.

Cope held out his card. "Copernicus Oursa to see Mister Haywood."

The secretary glanced at the card, set it down, and started to turn away. "He's tied up today and can't see you. You'll need an appointment."

"Tell him I'm here about Samuel Pearson."

The man hesitated, turned back. He looked at Cope with interest. "One moment."

As he went down the hall he said over the shoulder, "Wait here." Not that Cope was about to follow him. The greater the distance from that bruiser, the better.

No seat was offered but Cope took one anyway. He picked up a union newsletter which screamed of miners being harassed by owners. Mine owners were all the same, out for miners' blood. At least according to the union this was the case, whether in Cripple Creek, Idaho Springs, Carson City, or any mining camp. The blood sucking millionaires were to be resisted and fought wherever they were found.

A few lines into that Cope decided the Western Federation of Miners needed some writers on staff. He smiled at the thought.

A tall man, bigger and better dressed than the secretary, appeared, watched for a moment and spoke.

"As you read that I hope your smile is at the thought of company goons being busted in the chops."

He held out his hand. "Bill Haywood, Oursa. Good to meet you. Come on back. I'm not to be interrupted." This last was said to the secretary who had followed him out. The bruiser was careful to note the cordial reception given the visitor.

The office wall was covered with fine photos of miners working, pulling wealth from an unwilling mountain. Haywood took a seat behind his desk, perusing Cope's card.

"Have a seat. So. I see you write for De Volksstem out of Pretoria." He fixed a stern look on his face. "Didn't the British recently take Pretoria?"

"That is what my editor tells me, yes. I just found that out. Word is slow coming out of that part of the world. I can confirm that the paper is still printing!"

"Indeed. Nothing good happening there for the working man."

'You don't know the half of it, Haywood,' thought Cope.

"So true. I'm here, not there. I am a Boer. And I want to do what I can for my people. My family, I have learned, is destroyed, in camp or dead. Farms are being burnt, livestock slaughtered, people killed or sent away."

He paused, looking miserably and earnestly into Haywood's eyes. "Really, I need to…"

The miner finished the sentence for Cope.

"You need to talk to Sam Pearson."

Cope nodded, mute, swallowing anger and ashamedly fighting tears.

Haywood ignored Cope's show of emotion and displayed some of his own.

"My God, some things never change. I hate how the powerful have to smash anyone in their way. I see it in the mines and mills, and I see it in your war." A faraway look in his eyes and an angry frown fleeted across his face.

"You are in luck, my friend." He smiled, unexpectedly. "Sam Pearson is due here any day. He has been up in Wyoming and Montana. He delights in dogging the British buying officers. Speaks to the farmers before or after the Brits make their pitch to buy horses. Tells 'em not to sell to the imperialists. That sticks in those limey craws, I'm sure! But he is coming here to Denver to organize resistance efforts. That means, meet folks like you."

He stood, extended his hand. "Give my man out there some details of your situation—there in Africa—and local contact information. We will be in touch. To get you two together."

"Thank you. I'll get out of your hair. It looks like you have your own hands full fighting injustice and unfairness."

"Boy oh howdy do I. Good to meet you, Oursa."

"Call me Cope, please."

"You got it, Cope. Talk to my man out there."

"Thank you, Haywood."

The secretary expected the visitor to stop and talk. Cope gave just enough information to prove bona fides.

"I'm Copernicus Oursa. My father—same name—was killed on commando recently, not sure when. By marauding British soldiers. The farm is burnt. Mother, sister and brothers were sent to a camp. I need Pearson's help. I can help him as a reporter. You can reach me at the address on the card."

The man looked at Cope with a new respect. Cope noted it was quite different from the earlier, contemptuous up and down inspection.

"Thank you, Oursa. I'll see that Mr. Haywood gets this."

XII

Cope ambled almost aimlessly. He needed to go home but had a lot of ideas and information to think through. He walked twice as far around Denver as he would have going straight home. It was worth the time and exercise. He cobbled up a plan of action, or more accurately, a set of plans to pursue. First, Samuel Pearson. Second, Paul Piers-Read. Third, Licia Heldon and CPS. Fourth, Go see and publish information on British and related horse activities. Five, throw a wrench into those activities, on his own or with help.

Now, he thought, who is this Samuel Pearson fellow? Who is he, what is he doing, where does he work and live, is he really helping the Boers? Cope arrived home and got started. Putting on his reporter hat, he worked his contacts from all over. The east coast and Europeans gave him some ideas. He was primarily looking for Pearson. But if he saw an article or tidbit of information on other Boer sympathizers, he kept it for future reference. He knew but the avalanche of information again reminded of the sheer number of newspapers published in the US.

The next days were busy. He sent wires and bought drinks and 'was in the area so wanted to stop in and say hello.' Anyone who might know something or someone was fair game: old colleagues, his editor, new friends, competitors, you name it. The time was well spent.

One of his contacts, a retail clerk of some kind, surprised him. "Sure, Sam Pearson. Have known him for years. He was—is—my best friend, a neighbor growing up back east. He is an American, but also sports the stars of a Boer General. I saw my pal last month while visiting back home and he filled me in, with the war in the headlines and all. I guess ol' Sam works stateside. I think he is a real asset for the Boers."

"Oh really? What does he do here in the US?"

"Publicity mostly I guess. And he plants stories—or I guess he is a friendly source—for sympathetic reporters. I gather he also watches the British and their activities here in America."

"Activities?" Cope was pretty sure about them but was curious what the guy was hearing.

"Yeah. Buying horses and some arms and so forth."

"Really!?"

"Yes. Also, ol' Sam rounds round up supplies. For the Boers. And somehow ships them over there, how I do not know. The main thing, though is he tries to foster sympathy for the Afrikaaners and hostility for the British."

"Thanks. Most useful." He handed the guy a card. "If you hear anything else get hold of me, alright?"

The clerk smiled. "Sure, mister. Always fun to talk about old friends I knew back in the old hometown. Take care, and I will let you know if something comes up."

Cope did more research, working with a detective friend who told him: "He's a card carrying lawyer. Admitted to the New York and District of Columbia Bar. But I would think twice about having him defend me in court. His reputation and career are built on rabble rousing. Being a public gadfly. If you two ever meet up, he'll love you, being a reporter and all."

Things started to fall into place for Cope. Probably that was why he had connections with the Western Federation of Miners. WFM was not a middle of the road workers' group. It was a 'put up your dukes,' a do whatever it takes, aggressive kind of union. Cope guessed that Pearson and Haywood were cut from the same cloth.

He tried to follow the money but it was so convoluted he threw in the towel. How Pearson was funded God only knew and Cope decided he didn't want to. What he was doing with the money seemed chiefly trying to work American public opinion.

There were hints that the man was looking to take legal action against the Brits in the US. After all, he could file a suit for only filing fees, since he was a practicing lawyer. Another darker rumor wafted around Samuel Pearson. There were whispers that he was raising a group of enforcers to support his efforts. Cope thought Haywood's 'secretary' might be a candidate for that. And that Haywood probably knew of others who would be happy to contribute.

Cope did his best to shine a light on things. It was time to write and put up an article on the Royal Army and its horse acquisitions. He looked at the newspaper article on the British officer, memorizing Paul Piers-Read's face. To the source he would go.

HE HAD COLD CALLED IN A FAIRLY NICE OFFICE RECENTLY. AT that time he broke into sobs in front of that woman with the

Cruelty Office. That wouldn't happen this time. The news of his family was not fresh. The wound was still raw and tender, but at least no longer throbbing and bleeding. The dagger it sent into his heart fueled his anger and determination.

As Cope walked to the mission office he couldn't shake the image of his father riding away on what was to be his last commando. He straightened his shoulders, opened the door and marched in.

"Copernicus Oursa to see Major Piers-Read."

Again he handed his card to a secretary. She read it, set it down. This secretary was a woman, an American woman. He had never encountered a woman in such an important position. For a moment he found the very idea unsettling. But he realized she reminded him of his mother: middle aged, courteous but not to be pushed around, appropriately dressed, to the point but not brusque. He forced his thoughts from his mother as she spoke.

"Mister Piers-Read is not available. Actually he is out of the office and out of reach." She emphasized the 'mister' as if to hide the man's military background.

"When might he be back? Or reachable? I need to speak with him."

She consulted a notebook on her desk. "He will take appointments next Tuesday afternoon. Should I put you in the two o'clock slot?"

"Is that the best you can do? Nothing earlier?"

"No, Mr. Oursa, nothing earlier."

"Set it up then please. Two PM next Tuesday."

She nodded and wrote as Cope turned and left. Damn, he was ready to unload on this Engelse, and the guy wasn't even around. How irritating!

He stopped in front of the building, deciding what to do next. A speculative article! He'd write a piece asking leading questions to the readers. He wanted, hoped to force 'Mister Piers-Read' to respond. Cope smiled and turned to head back home. The office door opened and someone came out. It was the Major himself! Somehow Cope wasn't surprised that the guy had tried to avoid him.

"Major, I have a question. Can we talk?"

Piers-Read stopped and took the card Cope offered. Reading it, he frowned. Then he looked Cope up and down like a horse he might buy, glaring contemptuously at the same time.

"Anything I say will be misreported in De Volksstem. I'll not talk to anyone from that lying Boer rag."

"Afraid of the truth, are you? Then again I imagine you have plenty you don't want the world to know about. Or are you proud of burning farms and killing stock belonging to peaceful farmers?"

"Nothing to hide, Mr."—here looked again at the card—"Mr. Oursa. This office conducts legitimate operations with willing and honest businessmen. The authorities are aware of us and what we do, and we welcome honest coverage. Which, as I said, we won't get from De Volksstem. You have apparently heard rumors of burnings and so on. I do not know about what is or is not happening half a world away. My job is to procure horses here in America."

"Try me. How many horses have you bought so far? How many of them will survive the trip to Africa only to be shot up in your war of oppression? Do you tell your sellers about that?"

"You will have to read about us in your competitors' newspapers in order to learn about us. You are not welcome to ask us questions."

Cope saw red and his mouth ran away. "You cowardly son of a…"

"You can't talk to a British officer like that." The Major straightened and stepped in close.

Cope wanted to put a right to the jaw and a left to the stomach. But his temper cooled and words not his dukes did the jabbing. Even so, he did not step back.

"You are here to buy implements of war from a neutral nation. That is against US and International law. We will see that everyone learns of this, from shoeshine boys to Senators."

The Major relaxed, stepped back and grinned. "You fool. We're buying mules and horses from willing sellers."

"And we all know how those horses will be used. One of them carried the soldier who kill my kinfolk." He knew his tenses and grammar were mixed but didn't care. He glared. "And you will pay."

"Now you're threatening me? Go ahead, I look forward to this fight." The officer turned to walk away, stopped, turned back. "This is merely commerce, just business as usual, Mr. Oosik."

He looked again at the card. "Oh, your name is Oursa, not Oosik. My mistake, Mr. Oursa. And I am sorry for your kin, but we all have our jobs to do."

He strode away, not looking back. He was the very symbol of imperialism, a confident and powerful representative of a formidable Empire, able to work his will the world over.

Cope restrained himself, wanting to fly at the man, arms flailing. Instead he mulled different headlines and stories he could use. The man wouldn't talk to him. Cope determined to make the most of his avoiding the limelight.

The Major strutted off.

XIII

'REDCOAT INVASION!'

The screaming front page headline couldn't be ignored—the one inch type begged to be read. The newspaper lays on Licia's desk. She watched Gace's reaction as he read the article. He didn't need to pore over it; a quick read did the job. She had just put the paper down and was mulling it over. He glanced up as soon as he finished.

"So uniformed British officers are here buying up horses and mules. Or trying to, anyway. From all and sundry. And they are sending them to Africa to help the British fight the Boers. And it is run not commercially but with military supervision. The writer makes it sound vaguely conspiratorial or improper or something."

He sat and thought a moment. "I have to say I have seen no uniformed British officers striding around demanding their tea or saluting the Queen. Some men carry themselves like they just came from daily parade and roll call. So what? Good posture isn't a crime."

She smiled, thinking of other ways to describe that body language.

"Yeah, the uniform part is a stretch. But it does bring up some good points. There are neutrality issues, competition with our domestic needs and our Army, foreign officers operating on US soil, and so on. Isn't a foreign officer in civilian clothes technically a spy?"

"Yeah, I suppose so. A spy on a leash who everyone knows is out to gather what information he can."

She stood up and paced the office. "Did you see who wrote it?"

"Yup. Mr. Copernicus Oursa. The guy, the reporter who came to see you. I thought he was writing for some Boer newspaper, Volkster or something. He himself is a foreign national, whose loyalties are, shall we say, suspect at best. I wonder, how the heck did he get a piece in the Rocky Mountain News? And why?"

"Good question, Gace. The how, that is. The why? He has no love for the Royal Army who just killed his father and sent his family to an open air prison. His motivation is plain."

Still pacing. Licia went on. "I'd like to talk with him. If he can do that—get an inflammatory article on the front page of the Rocky—maybe he'll tell me how to get articles printed about the CPS. And, I want to find out how the animals the Brits buy are treated."

"Yeah. I don't want to pass up a good business opportunity. But I do have to think about the legal part of who the buyers are. And of how the animals are to be used."

Thoughtfully he looked again at the paper.

"This is the guy who broke down because of bad news from home, right?"

"Yes, I felt so sorry for him, crying in front of a stranger he had just met. It really got to him I guess."

"So, how much of this article is rage and reprisal versus solid research and facts?"

"Good question. Seems to be an interesting mix of both." Gace was curious. He had an idea.

"Licia, would you like to meet with him, the three of us? We can both get background and maybe learn the answer to that. And how, or if, it all affects the horse business hereabouts."

He backpedaled. "But first, how about you and I have dinner? We have plenty to talk on, this article and horses and other stuff. So, get with him not today but maybe later, in a day or two or something?"

"Yeah, I'd like to sit and talk with him, the three of us. And yes, Gace, dinner with you tonight sounds fine. When will you be by to pick me up?"

ACROSS TOWN, COPE WAS ORGANIZING HIS THOUGHTS AND going through accumulated mail. He shuffled through a stack of mail and notes delivered by messenger. Most had to be handled but many could wait a few days. There was an invitation to drop by the Cruelty Prevention Society's office. And then he saw a note from the Miners' union to go see Haywood. He didn't want to go see the 'secretary.' Cope truly hoped it meant Pearson was in town or would be here soon.

He set the partially opened stack down. He didn't care one way or the other about the CPS. Do-gooders, someone had called them. Seemed to him, they needed to get a job or something, not tell others how to run their lives. He felt a little ashamed he had broken down in front of that woman and didn't really want to go. He shook his head, clearing it. They might be an ally against the Engelse. They might have some way to get in and learn the British animal procedures. Then maybe they could help him give the British trouble about how they handled the animals.

But first he wanted to see Haywood. That would be time well spent, he figured. Over and above a contact with this mysterious Pearson. Maybe Haywood could recruit some union members somewhere along the way. Guys who ran and managed the transit or handling of British and other animals on the railroads and in the shipyards. They might well be able to give trouble or resistance to the Brits. Buoyed by these opportunities, Cope left and walked towards the Workers' hall.

As he entered the union office, he was treated differently than the previous visit. Clearly he wasn't considered just some slug off the street. He was someone to be acknowledged and respected. The secretary stood as he entered.

"Mr. Oursa, good you could come by. Mr. Haywood is in his office. Go on in, they are expecting you."

Knocking then pushing the door open, Cope took the room in. Haywood was closely listening while a middle aged man talked earnestly. Haywood wore dungarees and a work shirt; his guest sported coat and tie. The outfit was rumpled. Cope was no clothes horse but could see the outfit was old, out of fashion, and maybe a bit shiny from use. The man was dressed for business nonetheless.

The visitor stopped mid sentence and looked intently at Cope. The gaze made him feel as if the man could see all, his identity, his grief, his anger, fears, strengths and weaknesses...

Standing, the man extended his hand. "You must be Cope Oursa. I'm Sam Pearson. Good to meet you. Sit."

Haywood ignored the interruption and watched. The two Boers spoke a bit in Afrikaans, gesturing and clearly communicating, but there were no big smiles. Pearson glanced at Haywood.

"I was offering condolences, Bill. I never met his father but discovered that we have some acquaintances in common. But you need to hear all of this, and we'll stay in English now."

"I figured. Not a problem, Sam, go ahead."

"So, Cope, as your cousin said, I am a General in the Boer Army. I know and hate what they are doing to people like your family, and you. As an officer I am always looking for ways to help our cause."

He sat back. "I imagine you wouldn't mind throwing a wrench into the British works."

Cope nodded. "Of course I want to. But I'm not sure how or why a Boer General is here not over there. But I'll take any help you can give me. Truth be known, I'd rather be riding on Commando across the veld."

"So would I. But I can contribute much more here than I could trying to do that." He grinned sheepishly. "I can ride a horse but not well, and not for long."

Cope nodded. "I heard that a lot growing up. 'Contribute where you can, leave things a little better than you found them.' I will do whatever needs done from here, as little as that may be."

Pearson picked up the Rocky, folded to the article about the Redcoats. "Its not so little, my friend. Getting public opinion on our side is very important. This article is good. This is the kind of effective stuff we need. Can you do more like it?"

"Of course. But how does an article in a Denver paper make a difference? Can you get me more reach, broader exposure?"

"Yes. Send me any article you write for your paper or local outlets. I expect we can get play in other cities."

Pearson loosened his tie. "Now, young man. When you research your stories, I need you to go see what those Engelse are doing. Sure, visit their stockyards from time to time. But we also need the story behind the story. The more we know the better we can fight them. So, I want you to call on ranchers selling to them, inspect their yards and corrals, check on prices they pay, see how they treat the animals, and so on. And we especially want to know how many they are buying and shipping."

Cope nodded. In his mind's eye he saw a tall man strutting. "I've had a conversation with the guy in charge locally. One Royal Army Major, Paul Piers-Read. He's wearing civilian clothes, not his army uniform. I wanted to punch the stuffed shirt but held off. Maybe some day…"

Pearson smiled, shrugged. "I know some of those guys. Not him. For most of them, I know the feeling. Those Royal Army pricks think they own the world. They will get theirs, you wait and see. The sun is setting on their vaunted British Empire. Matter of fact, and maybe you can help with this. They have a camp with corrals and stockyards down in Louisiana. They gather shipments there before loading and sending them overseas, to Cape Town."

The mention of a scenic, pleasant African city, Cape Town, (not that he really liked any city), gave Cope a stab. He forced the pain down and continued to listen.

"We need to know what is going on there. Louisiana that is, not the Cape. Maybe—and this will have to wait a while, but think about it. Maybe a journalist needs to go take a look there, and make a report. Shining a light on them could give us a public boost. You know, foreign army base on US soil and all. Don't go off half cocked, but we will need you to go down there. Not next week, but fairly soon. We'll smooth the way for you."

Cope nodded but Pearson continued. "And we will pay the going rate for stories like this." He flicked the story in the Rocky.

They talked some more, agreed on a plan and how to communicate.

Pearson stood as did the newly relieved and energetic Afrikaaner. Haywood remained seated.

Pearson shook Cope's hand, gave him a card. "Send your articles and reports to me at this address. My people will handle the bulk of the work to get them distributed and so on. I myself will see some and will be sure they get wide exposure. For routine help, ask Bill's people here."

He looked at the miner who nodded, and then continued. "If you need to talk to me for some reason, contact Bill here. He can get in touch. But don't over use that channel, and don't say anything specific. The British are listening."

Haywood nodded. "And the mine owners and bankers and industrialists have their ears to the ground too. But hey, if you run across miners being abused, or hear about mine owners being in bed with your Royal Army, I'm all ears!"

Cope left and walked aimlessly, thinking and going over the meeting. So the guy was a General? He sure didn't dress or stand like one. But his plans and ideas made Cope feel positive for the first time in quite a while. It was a nice change.

Hungry, he headed to the first café he saw. Didn't know anyone or anything about it, but in his state that was best.

XIV

The café was half restaurant, half tavern. The air was thick and smoky. Tables were full. He saw there was one vacant barstool at the end of the counter. He went over, nodded to the person sitting there. "Is this taken?"

"No, help yourself."

From his open smile, Cope figured the guy wanted to talk. He did.

"The meat loaf is good today. Cook's special. And the parsnip pie."

"Parsnips? In a pie?" Cope wasn't sure but thought parsnips were akin to mealy tasteless carrots. Hardly pie material.

"Yes, the cook does wonders with workaday ingredients." A pause. "How about those Boxers in China? Thinking their religion or chants or something keeps them safe from bullets. Those guys have gone rampaging. Have killed thousands of Christians and westerners. Defenseless folks hacked or beaten to death. Those Boxers will find out about bullets soon, I'm afraid."

The waitress walked up and Cope motioned the meat loaf. "And I'll save room for the pie."

Smiling. "Alright. You're in for a treat with each of them."

Cope resumed the conversation on China. "Yeah, I read that six or eight European and western nations plus Japan are sending troops. I guess a Russian General is in charge of the task force. It will relieve the embassies and other places refugees are holing up. That won't be pretty. Those Boxers will be short work for the international troops."

The guy nodded. "Yes. When the Boxers' medieval superstitions meet the Gatling gun, guess which wins out?"

Cope continued. "I learned somewhere that the Dowager Empress is the last of the Manchurian dynasty which has ruled China for centuries. I read that her government is feeble and she has lost control of her nation. No doubt of that, it seems to me."

His new friend savored a bite of pie and went on. "Look for those foreign troops to stay in China for quite a while. The Europeans will force her to allow colonies or special zones there. Who is going to stop them?"

Another bite. "Troops are on the move everywhere on this tired old globe. The Russians have invaded Manchuria. The US has taken Wake Island out in the Pacific and made Hawaii a Territory. And the British have taken Pretoria there in South Africa, from the Boers."

For Cope the room went quiet. "Oh really. Do you know when that happened?"

"Nah, not exactly. But I have a lot of friends who are sick and tired of the British going in and taking places just to enrich their empire. Their 'Empah' as they say. Why do you ask?"

Maybe this guy was a kindred soul. At least Cope hoped so. It was a legitimate question.

"I ask because I am a Boer over here working. Word from there is spotty and not always reliable. Recently my father was killed on Commando and my family was able to get a letter out. They said there were going to be put in a camp after the English burnt the farm. So I..."

"My God, how can you stand it, being here?"

"Honestly I don't know. Wish I could wake up, be there, and fight, kill some damned Englisher. But I'm here and can't get back. The damned royal navy won't let people like me go back. Maybe I could go to the Belgian Congo and try to go overland. Good luck with that. I'm stuck here. And I will fight them any way I can. You say you and your friends are sick of the British?"

The man looked around. He was almost furtive, checking to see if anyone was listening or watching.

"I work in the stockyards here in Denver. And watch as the Royal Army buys horses and mules with their fat checkbook. And send them through our yards, after they accumulate a boxcar's worth they send them on. Cheyenne is their next stop. They must send them on somewhere, not sure. Myself, I haven't seen that yard, just heard from some buddies who have. I hear that those Royal Army guys treat the animals alright. Gotta give them that. But still. You have to wonder what is happening to..."

Cope interrupted. "First, how big is a boxcar? How many horses will it hold? And they go to Cheyenne, huh? Up in Wyoming, a hundred miles north, right? Are their yards in town or outside somewhere?"

"I probably said wrong. A boxcar can hold only eight or ten horses, at least safely. So probably they wait until they have a train's worth or something before sending them on. Friends tell me the Cheyenne yards are right by the train station, not outside somewhere. You can walk from the station. And trains from Denver run several times a day."

"Thanks. That is all good dope to know. Anything else about the Englishers I need to know?"

Cope's meat loaf and pie arrived. The man stood and readied to leave. "Nothing else I know. Hope it helps you. Hey, I enjoyed the talk. Best of luck to you. I hope you can find ways to put it to the Brits."

"Oh, I will. Thanks again for the info. And I hope the pie is as good as it looks, and that I can thank you for telling me about it!"

He thought on the conversation. Probably there were yards all over the west, accumulating horses and mules. Then sending them on to Cheyenne and who knows where else. Ultimately the animals ended up on a train for Louisiana, Pearson said. He decided he would have to go take a look.

GACE INTENDED TO CONTRIBUTE IN PART TO COPE'S PLANS. He intended to send Piers-Read as many horses and mules as he could turn up.

Early the next morning he hit the road. Visions of herds led him on as he climbed on to an eastbound makeup at Denver's Union Station. To Colorado's eastern plains he went. The Brits wanted farm raised steeds and pullers, not wild animals. They wanted the animals be at least semi broken and of course preferred they be saddle or yoke ready. It made sense to Gace to go where horses were born and bred.

The engine pulled the cars at a steady twenty miles an hour, pretty good progress.

The prairie drifted by, looking a lot like green seas. For some reason, Gace's thoughts turned from horses to his brother Ben in Cripple Creek. The man was big into being a miner and increasingly was a big union man. He sure hoped that work would not turn bad on his big brother.

His attention turned again to horses and mules, and he looked from the rolling green landscape to the people in the car. The man seated next to him looked familiar somehow. It was Charles Owens, the Byers rancher.

"Mr. Owens, I'm Gace McNall. I talked with you a while back about buying horses and mules. At your fine home south of town."

"Ah yes. You, Katherine and I sat and talked. I wondered where you had gotten to, not hearing from you and all."

"Well, like everyone things get busy for me. But here I am now!"

Owens smiled. "Quite. We have some horses you may like. Can you come visit today? We'll get you out on the prairie. See how they live and their condition."

Gace was glad he didn't have to wangle the invitation. "Sure, that would be good. I like riding the prairie and definitely want to see the herds." The train rocked along. Owens looked ahead and after a moment Gace broke the quiet.

"Say, I have a question. Is the town named after William Byers, the first owner of the Rocky Mountain News?"

Owens smiled. "You do your research and preparation, don't you? Yes, it was originally something else but when the rails came through it was changed. Byers is the trade center for many miles around. I had a tavern there in town for several years. I sold it and got into ranching. The hours are longer but freer, with no cleanup and daily restocking. And I am constantly in wonder how prosperous and productive the country can be."

They watched the prairie slide by, each in a sailor's reverie since it was almost like the sea in form. Rather than blue it was green and brown, rolling and endless. As the engines slowed, Owens turned and spoke.

"Now, when we arrive you ride with me out to the house. We'll have Ted take you out to view the herd."

XV

Ted Moore stood on the porch of the Owens ranch house. The ranchman looked out. The view was comfortable and familiar. Any more he hardly saw Pikes Peak lurking on the horizon to the southwest. He looked over at the visitor. The guy lived in the city but wasn't a dude. He was in dungarees, long sleeved shirt, cowboy boots, and Stetson.

"The herd was out along Bijou Creek this morning. Let's head there."

He glanced at Gace who shrugged. "Sure, let's go."

Ted told Gace, "Your horse is Polly. Say hello first, look her in the eye. Give her her head and she'll look after you. If you try to guide or manage her every move you'd better lookout!"

Gace nodded. He was used to sizing up an unfamiliar horse while it did the same thing to him.

The steeds were already saddled up. The two got on. Ted took one look around, reined his horse and trotted off. Polly wasn't about to be left behind and shortly caught them up. Gace realized Ted was right. The horse did know the routine and the land and was comfortable with him, so he held the reins loosely and looked around. They were side by side. Ted gestured.

"They're down there, I see them. We'll be there in a few minutes."

Gace marveled. "This bowl of sky you live under is huge. Being out here makes me feel small. In a way it is like being down at the bottom of a mineshaft, looking up. In there you feel like a spider in a big dark room. Here, it is almost like riding a rowboat in the middle of the Atlantic."

Ted smiled. "Yes, you have to be aware out here. Of course for you, Polly will take care of you. But coming out day to day, you can't take it for granted. There are few landmarks. Mostly you have to watch the shadows and turn around every so often to see how the weather looks. And to see how the view will be when you return. Thank God for Pikes Peak down there."

He nodded to the south and west. "On a cloudy day or in a blizzard it is best, if you have to go out, to get near to the creek and follow it. Hard to get turned around if you keep the creek at hand."

"Yeah I suppose so. I wouldn't want to come out here in a storm, I'll tell you that. Speaking of the creek, this is it, no? Bijou Creek? And there are some horses." He reined up and watched. They looked strong and healthy, and a little wary. "I'll take as many of those as you can round up for me. Yearlings and older, up to eight years."

Ted shrugged. "Fine with me. You need to tell that to Mr. Owens." A pause. "Is it the British Royal Army buying?"

"I'm not supposed to say." He smiled. "But yes it is the stiff upper lip crowd, and you didn't hear it from me."

"I thought so. Word has it they are scouring every ranch in the region."

Gace nodded. "Lots of folks are looking for horses. And mules. Them and the US Army are scooping up as many as they can. Of course, the Americans will just go out to northwest Colorado and round up wild ones. There are herds and herds out there and they'll take hundreds at a time. The Brits like farm or ranch raised horses for some reason. Easier to use and to load on a train or a ship, I suppose."

Ted cleared his throat. "A word of advice, Gace."

"I'm listening."

"Mr. Owens is Irish."

"That's it? He's Irish? So I should wave shamrocks or wear green or something?"

Ted smiled. "No, nothing like that. Just know that he and many others were pretty much run out of their country thirty or so years ago. Like many, he has done well here. He is American through and through. But I have to tell you, he has no love for the British."

Ted pulled up and stopped, surveying the prairie. He didn't look at Gace. "I didn't tell you this, right?"

"Tell me what, Ted?"

The young man smiled. Gace reacted.

"Oh. I see what you mean. Yeah, I remember being taught about the potato famine and all. So he or his family got lands taken and went hungry and all that?"

"He has never told me the details. I just know that Mr. Owens left Ireland with little and has worked very hard to be a success here."

"So, Ted, tell me. Will he sell to them? The Queen's Royal Army? I'm not wasting your time and mine, am I?"

"Not at all, this is not a waste of time. And yes, he'll deal. For a price. He'll sell good animals to them, no nags or cripples. But he'll get his fair number. And he will want to know the animals will be taken care of."

"Well, I'm supposed to bring buyer and seller together, favoring neither. But I have to say, when silver prices collapsed back in '93 I lost everything, everything. I know what it is to leave town and not know where to go. And to have your life fit in a suitcase, or in my case, a rucksack. So I will do what I can to get him a premium price. And certainly I can show that the buyer knows how to care for and maintain animals."

Ted nodded. "Fair enough. Let's go back to the house."

THE REST OF THE MORNING WAS PRODUCTIVE FOR ALL AROUND.

The afternoon train was on time. As he rode, Gace reflected. He and Owens agreed on terms. Gace was confident that the buyer would agree even if he didn't have the Major's specific approval. The herd would be picked up at Byers in a week.

Having the agreement gave him entrée. With permission from Owens to use his name, he spent the afternoon riding around to other ranches. More deals were struck, more pickups scheduled. He was glad he had taken the time to come east. When he got back to Denver he'd finalize the deal with the buyer.

GACE LOOKED FORWARD TO SHARING THE NEWS WITH HIS NEW friend, manager of Cruelty Prevention and would be investigator into Royal Army animal practices.

Licia smiled over a glass of wine.

"Sounds like it was a good profitable day for you, Gace. The next time you go out, though, maybe you could tell me. I'd like to go out there. Meet some of these ranchers and see their operations. I grew up on a ranch, you know, and likely I know some of them."

"I'll bet you do. Probably half the ranchers in Colorado know you. You cut a wide swath."

She made a face. "Do not. We know a few folks. But they are just family friends."

Gace's smile faded. "I'm not sure the two of us should call on them. Not together, at the same time. I want to buy. You want to schmooze and inspect. Different interests entirely."

"I suppose. But there's no reason we couldn't ride out to Byers together, make a day of it."

"Sounds good to me. I'll be going out in a week or so to supervise the herd pick up. Want to go then?"

"I think so. Let me check the calendar."

She took another sip of wine. "Say, you probably didn't see it but that Oursa fellow has another article. This one's not in the Rocky, but another paper. I think the Denver Times, but I don't remember exactly."

"Oh? So he's getting around. What does he say?"

"The headline is something like 'Why are Foreign soldiers on American Soil?' He asks why the Royal Army has soldiers here when we—the US—is neutral in their various wars."

"Good question. What are you going to order? I think I'll have the T-bone with vegetables and mashed potatoes."

DOWN THE STREET COPE TOO WAS EATING. HIS MEAL WAS about finished. He savored the parsnip pie, second go-round. First bite, he was skeptical. But, again, it was really good. He smiled at the waitress as he awaited change from paying up.

"Thanks, that was excellent."

Smiling, she made eyes. "Told you! I'll tell the cook."

Cope smiled. Maybe he should get her name. Then he had a better idea.

"Say, I'm a reporter. I'd like to do a small feature on this place. Alright?" They agreed he'd come the next day for an interview. Cope looked forward to writing something light and fun. The British shouldn't get all the publicity, he figured. He sauntered down the street, glanced in on a neighboring restaurant. There was that CPS lady, Licia. She was sitting with a man and they were laughing.

For some reason that sight made him sad and brought back his grief. Cope decided then and there that she needed to know about Paul Piers-Read. And his Cheyenne yards. And how the horses would spend hours on the train, scared and not knowing what was happening. He couldn't help it as he started to get worked up. Without thought, before he even knew it, he entered the restaurant and approached her table.

Gace glanced up at the man walking to their table. It was that Boer! He stood to meet him but the guy ignored him.

"Mrs. Heldon. Licia. I am so sorry to intrude. But I have learned things about the Royal Army and…"

She gave him a cold look. Her words, frigid, cut him off at the knees.

"Excuse us, sir. We are having dinner. Surely, whatever you want to say can wait. Why don't you come to the office tomorrow, ten AM. We can talk then."

Cope, deflated, nodded, turned, left.

Gace sat back down and grinned. "Wow. You take no prisoners, do you, Mrs. Heldon?"

"It is best to be direct. I am curious what he has to say. But not if he barges in over dinner. I assume you want to be there tomorrow?"

He nodded but she was looking at the menu and didn't see. "But enough of that. I think I'll have the lasagna."

Cope didn't sleep well. He spent hours planning his grand entrance to the ten AM appointment. He chose words and rehearsed then rehashed them even in his roiled dreams. He woke early, unrested. Even so he bathed and dressed carefully.

Finally he actually stood in the CPS' doorway. Going in, he saw the man who was dining with Licia. He didn't care and his spiel tumbled out anyway.

"The Royal Army has invaded. Not just my country but yours too!"

XVI

"...BUT YOURS TOO."

Terse and dramatic, the statement turned their heads. Cope had the floor, literally and figuratively. Ignoring the man, he zeroed in on Licia's eyes. And he made good use of her attention.

"The British Empire has officers here in the US. They are looking to buy horses. Horses and who knows what else they are buying. The excuse is the army has worldwide needs. Yeah. They need kill Boers and Boer livestock and burn Boer farms, not to mention what they're doing to the natives."

He paused. "Plus, not to mention all the other wars they are fighting to extend their control."

Gace thought this statement was over the top.

"The British are not invading. They—representatives of their Army—are here legally and publicly. They are here pursuing regular commercial transactions. No more, no less."

He extended his hand and asked, even though he knew the answer. "I'm Gace McNall. Who are you?"

"Cope, short for Copernicus. Cope Oursa." He wasn't sure how this guy fit in. Was he a friend or something else? "I have to say, you seem to know something about the Engelse and their work."

Gace took the invitation. He had nothing to hide, but was curious. "Engelse? What's that?"

"Sorry, sir. I am a Boer. Engelse is the Boer word for Britisher."

"Oh. Well, to answer the question you didn't ask." He smiled and went on.

"I am in the business of buying and selling livestock. And yes, the Royal Army is in the market for horses. And mules. So is our United States Army. For that matter, so are numerous freight companies, stage lines, race tracks, ranchers, and outfitters. To mention just a few. So what?"

Cope still wasn't sure of this McNall character was opponent, ally, or irrelevant. "And are you selling to the—what did you call them in your American revolution? The redcoats?"

"That, sir, is not your business. Speaking of which, just what is your business, Oursa? What do you do with your waking hours? Besides making accusations and so forth?"

Gace pretty well knew, but he too was trying to see if this guy was someone to be watched or relied on.

"I am a reporter for De Volksstem, a newspaper originally in Pretoria, Africa. About a year ago I was sent here to review American animal raising and care practices. I am interested in that." He glanced at Licia, hoping for a nod or smile which he did not get.

"I am of course still interested in that area of American life. But things have changed. The war at home has taken center stage. Everything is turned upside down for me, for many. I recently learned that the city of Pretoria and our editorial offices are now British occupied. Even so the paper continues to publish. How or where, I'm not sure. I just know that my articles and submissions continue to be printed."

Licia looked at Gace. "This is the man I told you about. He lost his father in battle and his family's farm is burnt and his mother and siblings scattered."

Gace sat and nodded sympathetically as Licia turned to address the visitor.

"Cope, take a seat. We understand why you don't like the British. But what do you think we can do about their being here? Like Gace said, it is all on the up and up, legally speaking. Let's all sit and talk about this."

He shrugged, and his accent came out in a rush. "There is no way to stop them being here. But their lives and efforts here can be made difficult."

This distilled Cope's thinking and being. "I can't go fight, can't carry a rifle or go ride on Commando. But I can and will shine a light on them with my reporting here. And I will learn all I can about their activities and stop or slow them as I can."

"Well now, pardner." Gace gave him a hard look. "What are you saying? Why should we help you interfere with or harm legitimate commercial activities? I understand you have a personal stake. I can't imagine being halfway around the world from home like you are. That said, you shouldn't go breaking American laws, abusing our hospitality. Or ask others to."

The two men stared, with neither offering an answer. They were not angry but held their position stubbornly.

Licia broke it off with a question for Cope. "Your reporting and stories are making waves already. Not just here in Denver. Your work is being printed in regional and even major city newspapers."

She picked up a paper and waved it. "Here's your byline in The New York Times, article sent by our head office. Pretty good for a correspondent to a little African paper."

Cope smiled and she went on.

"How did you get an article in the Rocky? And those other papers? I'd like to have that access for my articles about CPS." With her own smile she asked. "Can you help me with that? Give me a few pointers or ideas?"

"Yes, I'll give you a name." He thought a moment. "And I can introduce you. That's no guarantee. They won't just take just any article. The work has to be timely and relevant. I think I can get you in the door but then you are on your own." He looked at Gace.

"I don't want you or anyone to break laws." Cope swung to face him, not too close but earnest, even passionate.

"What we are talking about here is the most powerful empire on the planet, using their army brazenly. And they are hunting my people down like their fox hunts. And people—my father was one—are being killed just like the fox ends up! And others are thrown off their farms, scattered, imprisoned. For the love of God, why make it easy for them?"

Gace blanched, thinking of a fox, tired from the chase, cornered by a pack of dogs. Cope's images of his family brought the matter vividly, too vividly, to life. He looked at Licia then Cope, thought a moment then spoke.

"Alright, here's what I can do. I will continue to deal with all comers, Royal Army included. If they—the Brits—buy, I'll be sure they pay absolute top dollar. Of course I insist that every buyer treat the animals well. I will not break explicit confidences with them. Nor would I do so with you or anyone else."

The accent was still there but not so strong. "I wouldn't ask you to."

Cope nodded acknowledgment.

GENERAL PEARSON'S SHIP | 111

Gace noted that and went on. "But I can do this: I will keep you informed of what I learn. Of whatever is not specifically confidential or secret from them. I'll tell you what the Royal Army—and others are doing. Fair enough?"

Cope expected the guy to throw him out, not semi-cooperate. He nodded. "And likewise I will inform you—both of you—as I can. I am often bound by source confidence, but there is a lot I see that is fair game. This week I will go to Wyoming, Cheyenne, to visit their—the Engelse—yards where they accumulate horses for shipment. And to see whatever else I can learn."

Licia asked, "Engelse?"

"Like I may have told you, that is Afrikaaner for Englisher. Englishman or men. Limeys. Brits. Redcoats. The..."

"Oh." She interrupted his rant before he worked himself up with ugly word and thoughts.

Thinking quickly, she added, "I need to visit their yards too. New York will want a report. Plus I want to see conditions in the entire station not just the Brits' part. Wherever there are large groups of animals there is potential for mistreatment, disease, abuse. Usually there is proper treatment, but of course that depends on the people involved."

She looked at Cope. "The Engelse, huh?"

Then at Gace. "So, have you seen these yards run by the Royal Army?

XVII

Gace didn't know what to make of the fascinated look she gave the Boer when she mimicked his word.

"Yeah, Licia, I'm aware of these yards." Gace nodded. "In fact, I've got a ticket to go there myself, to Cheyenne. Bought it the other day, planning to make my own recon trip. I need to see the layout up there. Other buyers use the area as well. The Royal Army aren't the only ones who use the station area to gather animals. The big Midwest meat packers have a presence as do some big shipping houses."

She nodded in turn.

"Yes, that is a shipping point for cattle and lambs going east. As well as horses. Like I said New York has been after me to check the place out. I think they think it is a ten minute ride to get there, no idea of how big the west is. Anyway, this may be a good time. I'll get a ticket. How about day after tomorrow?"

Pleased and relieved for a moment, Gace relaxed. He was taken aback by her next words.

"Does that work for you too, Cope?"

"Nah. Thanks, but it is best that I go alone. So you two go ahead and make your own arrangements. You'll be there on legitimate commercial work. Not me. I will look around and could well skulk where maybe people aren't really welcome. Or I might even be up for making mischief, we'll see. But you didn't hear that."

Gace wasn't surprised the guy would be open to skirting the law. He sure as heck would if he had to somehow avenge his family. And he was glad he'd be going on his own to do whatever he had in mind to do.

"Didn't hear what?!" was his smiling retort. Cope grinned.

So did Licia, after a quick pause. "Oh. Alright. If there is anything I can do to help, Cope..."

Cope was grateful that someone cared. He knew she couldn't do much for him but he could probably help her out. The reporter in him came out. He pulled out his card and jotted something on the back. Giving her contact info was easier than trying to make an appointment, introduce the two, and so on.

"If there is a way you can help, believe me, I'll be in touch. Now, here. If you have a good story you want to get ink, talk to this person and use my name. He can't get every article printed but probably can help you with a good one. He's a good person to know in the publicity business in any case."

He smiled, extended his hand. "Gace, good to meet you. I hope you stick the Engelse for top dollar on every horse and mule. Or better yet I hope you find other customers and the poor Brits have nothing to ride. We should be so lucky, right? Anyway, Gace, we'll be talking I imagine."

Hand on the door knob, door partly open, he turned. "Thank you, both of you." And he left, a kick in his stride they hadn't seen before.

"Well," Gace said pensively, pausing. "A pirate sails off into the night. I wonder what he is really up to, and will be interested to see the papers in the next few days. I have to say, I really can't blame him for anger. And I certainly see why he wants to slow the flow of supplies to the invaders and wreckers of his home."

Lightening up, he smiled. "So, Licia, does Cheyenne the day after tomorrow still work for you, even if it is just you and me?"

"Yes. And don't get ideas. I just thought with three of us we could split up and learn more."

"That may be. But better that we stay on the right side of the law, and he won't is my guess. And truth be told, I'm happy to have you to myself for a day. We can do our own checking and then compare notes too. I want to see the RA's setup and I hear the US Army has a corral there as well. Plus like you say lots of other livestock goes through there."

GACE ALWAYS ENJOYED A TRAIN RIDE. HE'D NEVER RIDDEN this stretch up from Denver. Like east, the country to the north was rolling. The rails climbed—Cheyenne sat at almost sixty one hundred feet above sea level compared to Denver's mile high. So the going almost felt like there was a perpetual roller wave coming. But it was green, at least for the season, not ocean blue. And the wave never broke over them, just stayed the same distance out front. It was mesmerizing to him as they chugged along.

She was thinking not of waves but animals as she broke into his reverie.

"How do you know the Royal Army treats its animals well?"

"I don't from personal experience, Licia. But think about it. They have operations everywhere, in all kinds of places and times. And they depend on horse power. If they mistreat or neglect their four legged friends, their efforts and their troops are in trouble."

"Sure, but I can tell you story after story about people who depend on their animals. They know they have to have them. But they still abuse and starve and beat the poor beasts. Some people are truly stupid."

"Yes, I have seen that. But the Brits and their Army have used horses and mules for centuries. They use horses to ride and pull cannons. Mules to pack supplies. And at one time they drove herds of cattle to feed from. Maybe they still do some places, I don't know. The point is, when it comes to livestock and horses, they know what they are about. You're concerned about treatment and cruelty, right? It isn't my business, but here's my opinion. Seems to me you ought to look harder at the smaller operations, the ones lacking the resources of the British Crown. They may or may not do so well."

"I guess." The mantalk about tactics and procedures and so forth made her sleepy.

She nodded off and was soon snoring, kind of a piffle-oink-groan rhythm. He watched her steady breathing. All in all, Gace realized, she was a fine foreground for the changing scenery.

After a while Cheyenne appeared. Licia woke, and ran through her day. She had an appointment; Gace too had a full day planned.

Their Afrikaaner friend, unbeknownst to them, was already in town, scoping things out.

Cope got there before sunup and made a beeline for the corrals. He hung around, trying to look like he fit in. Soon he got to talking with a yard hostler. That is what the guy called himself. He was quite a talker.

"I'm just a cowboy retired from riding the range. I work here in the yards, an easy, predictable day. Riding over miles of prairie is a thing of the past for me. At night I have a roof over my head and a soft spot to spend the night. Not alone, either! And in a bed, not a blanket roll. The best part is, I only work a regular shift, nine or ten hours depending on the load. And get this, I get a bonus if I have to work more than ten in any one day. I get one day off every seven. Pretty soft! Pay is decent too, three dollars a day."

Cope nodded. "Sounds like a good setup. There must be a lot of traffic here. I mean, to keep you busy and keep you working on such good terms."

"Yup. Lot of trains bring stock from north, south, and west."

Cope pressed a bit. "I hear this is a big waypoint for livestock shipping. Are there a lot of big buyers who gather horses for shipping on east or west?"

XVIII

THE HOSTLER PAUSED, SPOKE SLOWLY, LOOKING AWAY. "YEAH, this here Cheyenne has a big shipping depot. Lots of cattle and sheep going to market in Chicago and points east. You mentioned gathering horses. The only ones doing that big time are the Army and the British. I guess the Limeys are working for their army too."

He swung and faced Cope, standing a few inches too close for comfort.

"Why do you care? I don't like that accent of yours, which you try to disguise. Are you German or something? Who do you work for?"

Cope was sure if the guy had a revolver it'd be pulled out, cocked and aimed. He did not want the guy to get more hostile, so quickly and earnestly spilled. Father dead, family strewn God alone knows where, farm burnt. He talked about being stuck in the States and hinted at avenging them.

The hostler shook his head. "Oh, well, hell. Glad you told me. I'm still mad at the British for what they did to my people, the Irish. My grandparents came here starving from the potato famine. In the 1840s and 50s the British invaders exported food from Ireland to England and let my ancestors starve! So I understand."

He grabbed and shook Cope's hand, smiling. "But I sure am glad you ain't a spy. Don't know what I woulda done if you were."

"Me too. You looked ready to take a poke at me."

"I was, believe me."

"And I am glad you didn't. So where can I find the corrals the damned Engelse—my native language for them—use? How many horses come through, and where do they go, do you know?"

"West end of the depot, three or four corrals. The number of horses depends. Sometimes filling them takes a few weeks, sometimes a few days. When they have a trainload, the horses are loaded in cars which go east. A friend in the dispatch office tells me they are headed for the New Orleans area. From there? Who knows, the poor beasts are put on a ship and sent somewhere in their precious 'empah.'"

"Thank you, that is really helpful. I need to go take a look."

"Walk lightly now. They have security, ex-military I think. Those guys scowl and walk around like they're on palace guard duty. And I think they're armed. Be careful. And good luck!"

The depot yards in Cheyenne were large. There was at least one vast switching yard with engines and cars being moved and shunted. It was an important cog in the transcontinental railroad machine.

As they got off the Denver train, Licia looked around. "Wow, this is really big. More spread out but I'll bet it is just as busy as New York. I have an appointment with the superintendent, or an understanding I am to drop by when we get in. So let's meet at the passenger terminal at what, say, three? That'll give us time for a bite before the return."

Gace pulled out his watch, glanced at it. "Sure. I know some of the shippers here and I have some foremen's names too. Will mosey around, talk and listen. See you then."

THE SUN WAS OVER THE MOUNTAINS TO THE WEST. COASTING down into Denver, the train's clickety clack was a nice backdrop.

Gace stretched and admired the view. "This was a good day. I got a handle on going rates and time frames between buying and clearing them out. And how much stretch in the price there is if a buyer really wants something."

"I agree, t'was a good day. I got a tour of the facilities. You know, sometimes I think people tell me only what they think I want to hear. But I have eyes and ears to overcome that. Seems to me the managers keep the animals fed, watered, and sheltered. I have a few names to watch, but what do you expect."

Licia turned back to making observations and reminders, writing quickly and in her own shorthand. "These new tablets sure are convenient. This one has lined paper stacked an inch or so thick, and the stack is glued on one end. So I don't have papers flying all over."

"That is easy to use I'm sure. Haven't seen that before. The things people invent!"

Cope skulked all day in Cheyenne. He was tired and hungry and looked for a café or an eatery.

The yard hostler, nursing a beer, looked up as Cope came in. "Well, its my spy! Did you find the corrals? How 'bout those security guys, really something, ain't they?"

"Yeah." Cope sat, motioned to the barkeep for beers. "For me and another for him too."

He stretched, smiled. "Just hearing those guys with their nasal British talk makes me want to puke. And then rub their noses in it. Hey, is there a way to turn those horses loose, get them out of the yards and free out of town?"

The man was so quiet Cope wondered if he heard. He stirred, looked around, motioned Cope to lean in, and spoke low.

"I've wanted to do the same thing. Damned limeys make me see red, I don't know why. When I see them I have to keep my hands in my pockets or I'd try to clobber somebody. So the answer is, yes, there is a way."

A way? Oh, Cope realized, excitement building. Letting the horses out.

"Will you help me? Or can I do it alone?"

XIX

"Will you help me? Or can I do it alone?"

Those words took Cope down a fork in life's road. Looking back, he wondered how things would have gone with a different answer.

The hostler—for some reason Cope thought of him as 'Hoss'—looked around furtively. Making sure no one was near, he nodded slightly. He uttered words between a whisper and a mutter; Cope had to strain to make it all out.

"There's a way. I will describe how to stampede the horses. Once only, talking and pointing only. I will not touch a gate or horse or person. And if you say anything about this to anyone, I will deny it. And then me and my friends will come hard after you. Is that clear?"

Cope took a long draining draw of beer, set the mug down. "Clear as can be, Hoss. I don't want to know your name nor you, mine. I'll call you Hoss. Drink up then let's you and me go take a look."

At first Cope thought his hostler friend was either drunk and faking an answer. Or maybe Piers-Read had somehow gotten to him and the guy was trying to set him up. That opened up a whole new set of worries, and also story themes he'd have to look into.

But as they walked, Hoss made good. He would point or gesture, and mutter. Again, always just loud enough to be heard, if Cope cocked an ear and paid attention. To others the guy just seemed to be mumbling, thinking aloud.

"Them guards leave this stretch unwatched the first twelve or thirteen minutes of every hour. They make regular circular rounds. You can time the trains by it." "That gate creaks noisy unless you open it real slow." "Spring that gate open just a little , leave it ajar and open it away so when they run, it swings open." "Then come here. Clap your hands or better yet or jangle a set of spurs, to set 'em on edge, make 'em run. If you can, punch the lead stallion on the nose, make him mad. Careful with that! Then, open this gate and they're gone." "Do it right and it'll take week to round 'em all up."

Hoss looked Cope in the eye. "You got it? Any questions?"

Cope shook his head. He had paid close attention. "No questions. Got it. Thanks, Hoss!"

They returned to the café but didn't enter. The man said, "If I see or hear that you've done it, I'll let friends know. Maybe they'll go out and turn out whatever horses are still around. Make it even harder for those limeys to round 'em up. Good luck."

No hand shake, no smiles, they just turned away, each intent on his errand.

Cope walked the route again, casually, paying attention to the shadows. He didn't see anyone who had been there earlier. No one seemed to be following him. He rememorized the layout and security. Then he caught the milk run back to Denver.

It stopped at many a little crossing. But the ticket was cheap and he intended to sleep the whole way. But he couldn't.

His mind raced. He went over and over the layout and gates opening and horses running. And he wondered. If he was able to empty a corral, what difference would it make? So what if the Royal Army had to hire a couple of cowboys to round up some horses? That wouldn't take but a day or two. The Engelse war effort wouldn't miss a beat, and the troops in Africa or wherever would never know. Maybe it was a waste of time…?

At one stop he saw a car, a railroad car sitting lamely on a siding. A wheel had somehow come loose. An axle sagged crazily, dug into the roadbed. The car itself looked off kilter. Cope watched as a crew removed the cargo. There were bags stacked in the car. The contents could have been coal, pinto beans, sugar, anything. The men had a line, rhythmically handing the sacks from one to another down the line, putting them in another car. Whatever the cargo, it wasn't too heavy since they were almost tossed hand to hand. In any case, the train and its cargo was going nowhere fast. Maybe, Cope thought, he shouldn't fool with the corrals. Maybe he should find a way to disable the train.

He couldn't stop the British. How could he draw attention and put at least a dent in their efforts?

"Was your trip to Cheyenne useful, Licia?"

She was surprised. When he left, talking of skulking, she figured he would drift into the shadows and not be seen again.

"Actually, Cope, yes, it was. I met folks and saw how they do things. Saw lots of animals milling around. I even got an idea about security up there, such as it is. You?" She smiled. "Did you skulk successfully?"

"I guess. I met some interesting folks myself." He thought of Hoss, gesturing and muttering, showing a pathway to temporary freedom for the horses. He brought himself back. "Tell me, is it healthy for a horse to be tied up in the dark and not have exercise for days?"

"No. They need activity and attention. Why?"

"The Engelse cram horses onto trains and send them to New Orleans. That trip takes at least three days, sometimes more. Then the horses are put on to ships, down in the holds. When a ship fills, it is sent to wherever in the world the Limeys are killing local people. Africa, India, they don't care."

She thought back to a ferry ride she once took in New York. The waves, the pitching, the inability to stand and even to sit still. Up on deck, in daylight and fresh air, she was able to withstand the half hour ride. She shuddered to imagine the horses' lives. It would be weeks of unceasing motion, crammed down in the dark, tied up, scared and uncared for.

He broke into her unpleasant memory. "The horses are not treated particularly well on their way. When they get to Africa the survivors, the horses that can stand and move, are ridden to the sound of the guns."

Cope turned to leave.

"Cope. Wait. How do you know this?"

"I observed the operations. I asked questions. Not of the Paul Piers-Reads. He thinks and believes what he wants to. As usual you have to go talk to the men in the pens. That's how to find out what's real. And, I was able to get myself a look at and tour of the corrals. And I know people."

"I'll look into this. Thank you for telling me."

XX

Cope needed to get this information to Pearson. He might know it already but better to confirm it than make folks guess. He headed to the WFM headquarters.

"Mr. Haywood is out of the office. Leave a message if you want and I'll see that he gets it." The secretary looked satisfied at that. Cope had a better idea.

"No, no message. Just tell him I came by. Thanks."

As he walked away he thought of how to word a query to his editor. The story idea was dumb and a non-starter, Cope knew that. But he hoped, intended, that it get passed up to Pearson. Who would read between the lines and know it was a request for clearance not an article being pitched. He turned over ideas for the wording and by the time he got home he had it.

'Propose a what dash if story stop Horses in corral awaiting shipment to war get loose and stampede stop Describe aftermath stop Should I pursue stop'

After sending the telegram Cope went home. It was afternoon but he was bushed. He fell on the bed and slept, uneasily. He dreamt of Licia. Of horses trying to escape an eddy, being pulled down by a sinking ship. Of him and Hoss in jail. Of explosions. Or was it cannon fire?

It was afternoon, and light on the prairie was exceptional. The shadows were starting to appear and lengthen, a magical sight. Gace was in Byers. He looked out the parlor window. Far to the southwest the mass of Pikes Peak loomed. In the foreground were corrals full of horses. Ted Moore was directing cowboys as they readied to drive the horses to the train yard in town.

Owens and Katherine Moore sat across from him.

"More coffee, Mr. McNall?"

"No, thank you. Those are healthy, strong horses you are selling."

Owens nodded. "Yes, they are fine animals. They are born and bred on the plains and will thrive wherever they go."

McNall smiled. "And well they should. You commanded a premium price. I have to say, now that the contract is signed, that I am surprised the buyers agreed. "

Moore chuckled; Owens smiled. "From what I read, the Boers are giving the Brits a run for their money. The invaders need all the help they can get. The Royal Army knows good horses when they see them. And there is no one to whom I would rather charge extortionate prices! It is only fair that I am getting a little bit back of what they took from me and my family. But that is neither here nor there." He shook his head. Gace felt it was to clear unpleasant memories. Owens went on.

"We raise sheep here as well, keep us in mind for that."

"I do have buyers but they'll not pay too high a price, Mr. Owens."

The seller laughed, stood and extended his hand. "I only ask a fair price. It was good doing business with you, McNall. Keep in touch."

AS USUAL GACE ENJOYED THE TRAIN RIDE OVER THE ROLLING green prairie. Tracks ran straight into the setting sun, twin golden arrows on the ground. He was excited and couldn't wait to tell Licia. He had several cars full of horses headed to the RA corrals in Cheyenne. Several corrals worth, he thought. Rancher Owens had come through and there were others in the area who would or already had.

Gace sat back, relaxed. The image of his horses corralled in Cheyenne and Cope 'skulking' up there made him realize that Cope and Owens had much in common. Both had reason to dislike the British. It was a passing thought. There were many folks who didn't care for the British, so what? He had plenty of his own work to do. He needed to get these horses delivered to the Royal Army and receive payment.

BACK IN TOWN, COPE TORE OPEN THE TELEGRAM. HE HADN'T expected such a quick response. It wasn't from the editor but from Pearson. And it was the response he hoped for.

'Write story stop Particular interest the aftermath stop Plan on coming to see me NOLA stop Pearson

'NOLA'? What did Pearson mean? Oh, New Orleans Louisiana. His home base, of course.

That mystery solved, Cope realized he had set something big in motion. He hoped it wouldn't swallow him up, but in a way he didn't care. He looked forward to returning to Cheyenne. Doubts again raised their frowsy heads. They were replaced by an image of a laughing Engelse in front of a burning farm house. He straightened his shoulders and forced that image away. In its place he drew a mental image of confusion, horses running, people yelling. Of some horses escaping to the high plains

Now, to create just such a reality.

"Hello Licia." Cope had waited outside patiently while Licia spoke with some woman. She looked familiar, he wasn't sure how or where. At length she escorted the visitor to the door. "Ella, thank you for your concern. I will look into it."

She rolled her eyes at Cope as the woman walked away. "Ella Queue. A true animal lover, she really is. But she is not all there, if you know what I mean. One of those always ready to burn down the house just to get rid of a pile of dirty dishes, if you know what I mean."

He looked stricken.

"Oh my goodness, Cope. I am so sorry for that expression. That was thoughtless of me. I just meant she is ready to make trouble with the slightest excuse."

"No matter."

"How are you, Cope?"

He smiled. "Good. I'll be going back to Cheyenne soon, as soon as the corrals are full there. Do you want to come?"

"Why? When the corrals are full?" She tried not to smile. "Cope, tell me you're not up to something. Sure, you're angry but don't go do something to get in trouble."

A crazy idea came. "No, actually I was making a joke. Forget it. I just wanted to stop in and say hello. Maybe when things settle down and all maybe you and I can have dinner. The editor gave me an assignment so will be busy for a while. When I'm done I will stop in and maybe…"

"Oh Cope, I am really busy these days. Maybe some time, let's talk and see."

"Alright. I'd better get busy, and will leave you to your work. See you later."

He was relieved to see that he wouldn't have to chase the Ella woman down. She was nearby, and to Cope she seemed to be 'all there.' She sat easily on a street side bench, and watched, flat eyed, as he approached.

"Hello Ella. Licia at the Cruelty Prevention tells me you love animals. I'm Cope. Can we sit and talk a little?"

XXI

THE CLOSER THE MAN CAME THE MORE WARY ELLA FELT. HE stopped, stood near and talked to her. She was aware and grateful that they were in full public view with plenty of people around. She scooted to one end of the bench and motioned to the other.

"I don't know you. But you can sit if you keep your distance. Go ahead, sit. I'll scream if you try anything. Cope, you say?"

He sat, crossed his legs, and put an earnest expression on his face.

"Yes, Cope, short for Copernicus." He laughed. "Licia said you like to solve problems. In a big way. That is good, Ella, I like that." She stiffened, ready to get up and walk. "Please, Ella, take it easy. Relax. I just want to talk about animals. And helping them."

A guarded smile. She made the tight muscles in her shoulders go slack, a little bit anyway. "Animals... Well, go on."

A few hours later, after a meal, she sat back, full and content. But not happy.

"So these horses are taken to a corral, packed in and forced to stand and wait. Then they get stuffed onto rail cars and sent east. And then stuffed into a ship and sent to war. A war you have a stake in."

"That's about it, Ella, yes." Cope looked her in the eye, ready to ice the deal.

"Can you keep a secret, Ella? For me and the sake of those horses?"

She nodded. "Yes. I will tell no one."

"If I told you of a way to let those horses loose, give them a fighting chance to get away, would you believe me? Would you help them and me?"

Ella brightened. "Well, yeah, yes, I would. Tell me how're we going to do it?"

"Cope came in the other day, Gace. He stopped in just after I finished up with a visit from Ella Queue."

"Ella Queue?"

"A local animal rights worker. You met her, remember? She is one of those people who is always ready to go to battle. She is a good information source. But she is too ready to put up her dukes for my taste."

"Ah. Better to know what she is up to than not, right?"

"Yes. Anyway, I was getting Ella out of the office when he stopped by. Had to talk with her and listen to her craziness for a while before I could ease her out. When he came in he looked kind of wound up. Made some comment about how he'd be going to Cheyenne when the corrals were full."

Gace's ears tingled at that. He knew his shipment would be filling the corrals in the next day or two. He wondered just what Cope might be up to. "Oh? Did he say why, give any reason or anything?"

"No, but he looked thoughtful and almost smirky.

"Smirky?"

"You know, almost as if he had a secret he wanted but didn't want to share."

"Oh."

She rolled her eyes. "And I questioned him on it. Kidded him about not making trouble. That made him be real serious. He said nothing was up, he was just curious. Then said he had work to do and left."

She paused. "You know, I made mention of Ella being an animal rights activist. But an activist always wanting to put her dukes up. Always ready to go to battle at the drop of a hat. He seemed to ignore that, but he sure boogied out of here in a hurry. It is hard to tell with him."

"True that."

"And sure enough, a minute later, just before you came in, I glanced out the window. Cope and Ella were sitting down the street on a bench, talking earnestly".

He snorted. "Let's see, we have a man angry about the British and their war horses talking to a woman angry about animals and life generally. That was an interesting talk, I'll bet."

"Yes, Gace, I would love to have heard that!"

"Hmm. You know, at least I think I told you, I was able to arrange for rancher Owens, out in Byers, to sell several hundred head to the Royals. Shipped in to Denver yesterday and today, to be sent on to Cheyenne tomorrow."

They looked at each other.

"You don't think this is all tied together do you, Gace? Cope and full corrals and Ella and your shipment?"

"I don't know. I hope not. Either way, I am scheduled for Cheyenne tomorrow. I'll find out then, I guess. Do you want to join me?"

XXII

"Tell me again Cope. Why do we have to ride last class? These benches are hard and really crowded." With that Ella elbowed the woman sitting next to her.

"Move over, you cow. You're on top of me."

The woman elbowed her back. "Listen fatty, I paid for my space, so if you don't like it, go somewhere else." She fluffed her skirt and looked straight ahead, ignoring everyone.

Ella was ready to get up and make a stand. Cope lightly tapped her shoulder.

"Ella, I told you why. We want to get to Cheyenne on the sly. Which means don't make a scene. No trouble."

He looked at the woman and back to Ella.

"Alright, Ella? Are you with me? We don't want anyone, especially the horse dealers and the Engelse to know we're there. If you pick a fight we'll get thrown off this run. The train crews will gossip and word will get to the livestock handlers and we'll be sunk. Right?"

Ella realized he was right. What were they going to do anyway? Oh yeah, something about saving horses. She was all in with that.

"Engelse? What's that? Oh yeah, you told me. He's the British guy in charge. Paul Pary Reese or something. And you are right, Cope. I'll settle down. We don't want trouble here on the train, I agree. Sorry, she just riled me, sitting there in my seat space, acting all calm and in the right."

Cope thought two things: the name was almost right, and good, she won't make a scene. He was beginning to regret getting this kook involved. She needed to be watched every second or she'd go off the rails. If she had ever been on them. At least she could take the blame if things went bad.

"The man's name is Paul Piers-Read. Yes he is the one in charge of British horses and their handling. If you had met him like I have, you'd agree, he is a stuffed shirt."

Ella laughed. "I hate it when people think they are sooo important."

"He does that. And believe me, Ella, we are going to unstuff this guy tonight."

She giggled. He stopped, thought. "You brought everything I told you to, right?"

She rolled her eyes and nodded. "I ain't dumb, you know? Of course I did. Its all right here." She picked up her full carpet bag with effort. "See."

A man entering the car caught her eye. Her gleeful cockiness evaporated. She quickly slouched down, faced the window, and pulled her jacket up.

The man stopped. "Well, hello. Cope Oursa. How are you?" He extended his hand, shook Cope's. "Cam Braun, the railroad guy, remember? You never looked me up to see how we treat our animals in building the railroad. Too bad, I was looking forward to showing you."

She couldn't help herself. "Hey Braun, I have seen how you treat your horses and mules on the railroad. It is terrible!" She looked at Cope. "Don't believe a word this man says. He..."

Cam took a step back and laughed. "Well, Oursa, you have fallen into strange company." He looked at Cope as if assessing his character. "Trouble follows this Ella woman like rats after the pied piper. Be careful. If you—not you two but you, Cope—want a tour, come by the Denver office."

He spun and left.

Cope took a hard look at Ella. "So much for slipping into town. That man knows railroaders everywhere. I bet he's already telling his buddies about the crazy woman in car seven. You better get off at the next stop."

"You're stuck with me, Cope. This is an express run. We're on for tonight!"

"No, we are not. I am but you are getting off. If I have to, I'll pull the emergency. And I will make sure you do get off."

"But what about stampeding the horses? What about our plan?"

"My plan. You get off when we stop and go back to town. Denver. And if you breathe a word of this to anyone you will regret it. Keep it under your bonnet, do you understand?"

She glared but nodded. "Oh alright. I hope your plan backfires and you end up riding somewhere with the horses."

He stopped the conductor.

Licia glanced out the window. "I wonder why we're stopping. I thought this was an express run. Look, there's Ella. She is getting off. Alone. The conductor is seeing her down the stairs. She has no baggage and looks more upset than usual. That's saying something! How strange." She watched, wondering.

"Hmmm. I wonder if Cope is involved somehow? Look, he's at the car door, gesturing and talking and she's talking back. We've started up and she's running along, yelling. The conductor is pulling Cope in to shut the door." Gace got up. "I want to talk to him."

"Wait for me." She joined him and they walked back.

COPE STARED OUT THE WINDOW. CATTLE AND HORSES DOTTED the country. They grazed, ignoring the giant noisy smoky engine pulling cars. The peaceful scene was opposite of his emotions. He raged. Of all times for Cam to stop by. And at Ella for mouthing off. What else should he expect? He hoped she did go straight back to Denver and kept her mouth shut.

That somehow brought to mind that the Engelse were gathering horses to use to kill his relatives. He would stampede them if it was the last thing he did on this earth. He had to avenge his father! Lost in images of running horses, he didn't hear people approaching.

"Cope. I saw you talking to Ella yesterday. After you left the office. When you threatened to go to Cheyenne 'when the corrals were full.' Now here you are on the way there, and Ella just got kicked off. Can you tell us what is going on?"

He looked up at Licia. Gace stood behind her, looking at him curiously.

He patted the seat next to him; she sat and Gace sat across from them.

Cope took a deep breath. The story came out, not in full detail but enough to explain. "This is a long and sometimes boring story. It is like this. I…"

Some time later, the train slowed to enter the Wyoming depot yards.

She shook her head as if to clear it.

"So you want us to help break or bend the law. You want to trespass, break and enter, lay hands on or interfere with someone else's property, and create chaos, possibly hurting people or horses in the bargain. Do I have that right?"

"All but the last part, Licia. The thing is to set the horses free, not hurt or harm them. And no people will be hurt. Well, I guess someone could be hurt if they step in front of the herd. Too bad for them."

Gace was angry and confused. Angry that Licia would even consider this, that she didn't flat out refuse. Angry at Cope for wanting to harm his customer and the stockyards in general. Confused that he felt some empathy.

Cope looked at him. "You can round these herds up and sell them again. The Engelse have more money than sense anyway."

Gace looked at his friends. Of a sudden he smiled, chuckled. His laughter roared. It was too good. Owens would laugh too, putting it to the British. Again.

"I can't help you do it, Cope. I don't want to hear any more about it. But I won't stand in your way. No way do I want to know details. In fact, we never had this meeting." With that, Gace returned to his seat in the next car.

Licia paused, knowing she was crossing a line. Her motivation was simply to save the horses so they could live out their lives under the Colorado sky. She didn't want to think of horses in the hold of a ship after a long train ride, then dodging gunfire in Africa.

She didn't, couldn't think twice about her decision. After all, she would be taking on a worldwide empire. And committing crimes. And endangering her future with the Cruelty Prevention Society. And willfully ignoring the reactions of her ranching family and friends. Not to mention how it might harm Gace...

"I will help. Maybe they aren't being mistreated, the horses. But they are being collected just like ammunition, to be used up in war. I want to do what I can to fight that."

XXIII

Later. Licia relived how a Colorado cowgirl, wanna be artist, and animal rights activist got here. Her thoughts drifted back to the day she and Gace saw Cope on the train.

On the train to Cheyenne when Gace walked away, she stayed with Cope. The decision made, she woiuld help free the horses. Actually, she knew they weren't going free. They would be sprung from jail for a day or two is all. But she liked the symbolism of it.

The Boer, accent coming to the fore with his excitement, filled her in: where in the yards to go, which gates to open, and so on. She couldn't wait!

Cope was talking. "We'll go tonight. Today, we need to lay low. We'll take a room, lay down, try to rest and gather ourselves."

The morning and into the afternoon, lay down they did. As for rest, not so much. Righteous frenzy was shared between the sheets.

ELLA HAD HOPED FOR JUST SUCH AN OPPORTUNITY WITH COPE. She of course didn't know about him and Licia. But one thing she did know, no one could dump her! Someone would pay for publicly shoving her off a train! She hooked a ride with the conductor of the next one through, giving him reason to be glad he did.

Her train had arrived Cheyenne and was not moving, waiting for a platform to open up. As they sat in the yard with engines shuttling cars around, men shouting, animals bawling, she tried to force a smile. After a moment it came on and lit up the cabin.

"And I need to get back to Denver this afternoon." Her tongue stroked her full smiling lips and she looked with warm eyes. That gesture melted him. He stammered. "My train leaves at 7:30 sharp, if you want."

"I do want. And I'll be back to see you before then." She brushed against him. "But I'll be gone for most of the day. I need to talk to some people. Do you know, where are the Royal Army corrals?"

THE SUN WAS PAST ZENITH, COASTING TOWARDS ANOTHER TRIP below the horizon. Cope stood, pulled on his new denim pants. Stray thoughts about them flew through his head. Levis, they were called, for the founder of the company Levi Strauss. He liked their look and durability. The copper rivets made it look like they'd last forever.

"Let's go walk the route. It'll be good for us both to see it in the day."

"Are you sure that is a good idea?"

"No one knows us here. Next time it'll be dark and no one will even see us. Get going."

"Who appointed you general in charge? Relax, we'll go. Give me a few minutes." She smiled, grabbed and pulled him down. More than a few minutes passed.

The route was pretty much as it was the previous checks. They rounded a corner near the target corrals. There stood Gace, facing away. He was talking to a tall and gawky man who could look up the way which he did. The man stopped mid sentence, eyes boring on Cope.

"You! You two! Stop!" His nasal British accent echoed and grated. Cope fought back an intense urge to rush and tackle the man.

Gace turned. The man he'd been talking with left and was stalking towards Cope and Licia. Gace unsuccessfully stifled an exclamation. The man stopped, turned.

"Do you know these people, McNall?"

"Yes, Paul, I do. They are simply friends who rode up to Cheyenne with me. Why?"

"I know this man. He calls himself a 'reporter.' But he is a Boer agent! And we were warned of an attempt to sabotage our yards. Tonight! Our information is that a man answering to his description will try to interrupt our operations. It is him, I have no doubt!"

Looking at the couple, he yelled. "Guards! Guards! You two, stop, I will have you arrested." He waved his arms trying to get someone's attention.

Cope took a step forward and laughed. "Arrested? For what, you officious ninny? Standing on a public sidewalk? Go ahead, call the Sheriff. I'm sure he'd love to hear your complaint. Go ahead, get him. He'll be interested when we tell him of a foreign agent harassing bystanders. Go for it, Major!"

He snorted and laughed again. Then slowly and contemptuously turned his back. "Come on, Licia, let's go."

Piers-Read rounded on Gace. "You associate with such people? I thought you were a gentleman and a friend. But you are neither if you acknowledge those people. It is best that you go with them. Go on, go away. I have to decide whether we want to do business with you."

Gace chuckled. "Your quota is unmet. You need me and my horses more than I need you, Read. Oh, excuse me, make that Piers-Read. Your quota is half full. You need horses and I have them. With access to many more."

The Englishman gasped. He knew that was true but could only sputter.

Gace stepped back. "It is time to reevaluate whether we even want your trade. I will consult with colleagues in the business. I may be in touch." He left, making a point of sauntering not fleeing.

Around the corner he saw the pair. "Well, that certainly did it up brown. Now they know you are here and are on the lookout. And the Major tried to send me packing. But I was already headed out the door."

"So now what?"

"I don't know about you," and here he looked at Licia, "but I am going back to Denver. Not sure there is any more damage I can do up here in Cheyenne!"

XXIV

Life's daily rhythms returned after they returned to Denver. Gace kept busy working to find new buyers and sellers. Licia wrote and rewrote reports about Cheyenne and the various operations there. Cope continued to dream and fantasize on ways to frustrate the British.

After reading the papers he went to visit Licia at work.

"Cope. You are out bright and early. What brings you by the CPS?"

"Bad news. Licia."

"Oh? Are you alright? You look upset."

"No, I'm alright. Not hurt or anything. The thing is, I got a visit from my contact. That sounds so spy-ish. She was an assistant editor, now a book store owner. You know, the one who helped me get my articles and so forth into local papers."

"Yes. I want to thank you again for that introduction. She and I have collaborated on some stories."

"Well, someone, probably that Ella, told her about the plan."

"The plan? Oh, yes, the plan to loose the horses. So now she knows you are doing more than reporting on animal issues for an Afrikaans paper?"

"I imagine she wondered, but now she knows. And she told me to expect no more help. Worse, she has told her contacts. Those two shes, Ella and the bookstore woman. They ruined me!"

Licia wrung her hands as if throttling a snake. "I wonder if she'll work with me now, knowing you and I are friends. Well, all I can say is, I hope Miss Ella comes in here sometime. I'd like to put her straight. If I get my hands on her..."

Cope was taken aback. He expected a brushoff, not empathy and vehemence.

"It'll be alright, Licia. Don't worry."

They looked at each other, wondering.

GACE WALKED IN HOLDING A NEWSPAPER. IT WASN'T THE Rocky, but the Denver Post, a less known rag. Gace enjoyed it's sensational headlines and positions. Talking, he looked at the paper not her.

"You and your buddy Cope cut a wide swath there Licia." He looked up.

"Oh. Hello, Cope."

Gace stopped, grinned, looked the two over. He held the paper up, pointing at an article.

"It says here, your full name is Copeland Ursus. What, did you change it? This Ursus fellow is accused, as you probably know, of trying to set loose hell on earth up in Cheyenne.

You know, don't you, that you are involved in animal cruelty, assassination, and vandalism. And conspiracy. And intended use of explosives. Not to mention spitting on the sidewalk. And that is just for starters!"

Cope smiled, wondered how someone mangled the facts so. Gace went on.

"Also it says that you're not a journalist but a Boer agent. You are paid in diamonds from the new diamond mines youall are fighting over. Can I have a loan? Seriously, you are accused of kidnapping a Denver businesswoman. And holding a a gun to her while you went north to Wyoming. And you intended to force her to aid and abet in your crimes? What a bad actor you are!"

Gace paused, smiled. "Plus you kick dogs and knock down little ladies."

He caught a breath. "The paper doesn't accuse you of the last, I made that up. Wow. Man, Cope, what happened? You have managed to make some big time enemies. And all you did to earn it is walk around some corrals and get a few news articles printed."

"Yeah, and I made the mistake of kicking Ella off the train and out of the plan. She was getting hinky and along comes a railroad guy I barely know. He knew her and said she was trouble. I acted on it, kicked her off. Boy oh boy, was he right! I should have kept her close and on a short leash, not made an enemy by shoving her out."

"Well, the Post reporter gives credit to 'a concerned woman citizen.' This woman got hold of the reporter and told of your plot to destroy the Cheyenne stockyards. At least that is what the article says you were going to do. And buried in the print the 'concerned woman citizen' is identified as one Ella Quay, a 'well known civic leader and animal activist.' So you're right, Cope. No doubt it is her. Bad move."

He turned to her. "And you, Licia. What are you going to do now, fair maiden in distress who was rescued by Ella's civic righteousness?"

"Me? I'll let New York know how things look up there. Not bad, really. And I'll let them know about this so called Copeland Ursus. It'll blow over pretty quick. After all we're out in nowhere land as far as they are concerned."

She kind of smiled, turned to Gace.

"But you, mister. You had better be careful 'cause you're not out of the line of fire. You were seen with and acknowledged knowing us up there. Your boy Paul Piers-Read isn't done with this, I'll bet. You may be next."

Cope threw his hands up in mock surrender. "I don't know what to do."

Soon he did.

XXV

Cope wandered home, not really wanting to get there for fear of... what? Actually he hoped that poor excuse of a man Read or Piers-Read or whatever his name was would be waiting. Or the reporter from the Denver Post. He felt like settling with either of them real quick. That'd be easy and satisfying. Not like fighting the British Empire singlehandedly, or seeing outright lies about you in print.

As he approached, things looked normal. There was no lurking officer, or British soldier, nor a reporter. But there was a telegram boy walking away. Cope called to him.

"Have you anything for Oursa? Cope Oursa?"

The kid turned. His skin was ebony. For a moment Cope was surprised, having seen few Western Union boys of African heritage. But he had grown up playing with black African kids, no big deal.

"Mr. Oursa? Telegram!" He held out an envelope, took the penny tip and grinned. "Thanks mister!"

Inside, Cope opened it. It was from Sam Pearson. He read and reread it.

'Congrats yr effort even if thwarted stop Your usefulness there done stop Have work for you nola stop Come soonest practical stop Pearson'

Cope looked around his room. So he was going to Louisiana. He would miss Licia and Gace and Denver's blue sky. But he wouldn't miss Piers Read and the lying reporters. He pulled out his suitcase, tossed it down. He made a mental list of what to take and what to leave but didn't start to pack.

HE RETURNED TO LICIA'S PLACE. WORKING AT HER DESK, SHE looked up.

"New York wants me to keep an eye on horse shipments, particularly military ones. Not that we can stop them but if there's mistreatment we can shine a light on it. I may have to go back to Cheyenne a time or two. Do you want to go with me?"

He sat. "Pearson wants me in Louisiana."

"Louisiana? What's there? Why? And who is this Pearson person?" She smirked at her wordplay.

He didn't react to it.

"Pearson is a Boer general working stateside. He is not Afrikaans but a sympathetic American citizen. He is actively opposing the Royal Army and their horse buying. And other war preparations here in the U S of A."

"Oh? He has kept a low profile."

"Not with the Brits he hasn't. You ask what is in Louisiana. There is a stockyards, a British corral complex bigger than Cheyenne. In Chalmette, near New Orleans. They gather horses there from all over. Ships are always coming in to port. They are loaded up and sent out."

He showed her the telegram. "He wants me there. I expect he'll have me doing more work like we tried up in Wyoming."

He paused, almost afraid to ask. He figured the worst she could do is say no, so went ahead.

"Do you want to go with? See how the horses are treated along the way, and how they go to war? It could be exciting, even dangerous."

She shuffled papers, stalling and thinking.

Gace came back in holding the latest edition of the Rocky Mountain News.

"I've got to stop reading the papers—all this news about supposed criminals and horses and the British is keeping me from work. But this is important, it could affect what I'm doing."

He folded the paper to highlight an article and showed it to them. "Look, some guy named Pearson is filing suit in New Orleans."

Cope looked at Licia, cocking an eyebrow.

Gace went on. "This Pearson guy is seeking an injunction. Why he cares I don't know."

"Cope was just telling me about this Pearson person." Licia deadpanned and this time Cope rolled his eyes before he jumped in.

"He is American but is an Ally of us Boers. And he is working to thwart the Engelse. I just got orders to go to Louisiana to help him."

Licia cleared her throat. Cope added, "And Licia is going with me. Maybe."

She averted her eyes, thinking and wondering if she wanted to go.

Gace was gobsmacked. "Orders? Licia? What…"

It was all too much. He simply shook the paper as if to re-find his place, and continued.

"He says the trade in horses and mules by the Royal Army violates the US Neutrality Act. Says such horses are intended and used as armaments of war, no different than ammunition or artillery. And a judge in New Orleans is looking at the motion as we speak. Not to beat a dead horse, but that could stop my business with Paul dead in its tracks. So to speak."

Licia and Cope exchanged smiling looks.

Gace paced, preoccupied, didn't see it. "I had better get busy, make some other contacts. Even if the suit is stopped I need other buyers. Can't depend on the limeys."

He started for the door, stopped, turned. "Say, Cope, what do you mean you got 'orders'? Since when did you take orders?"

"Well, Gace, I am doing what I can to avenge my family. And the farm they burnt and the sheep and cattle they bayonetted. And I want to, have to, make it hard for the Engelse. True, I am not a uniformed soldier. I'm not military but I am at war." His thick Boer accent came out as he said that last phrase.

Gace nodded, then speared Licia with a look. "And you. Are you going south with him? What about the CPS? What about…your friends here? What about me?"

Gace turned and left.

There was silence then Cope stood, walked to the door, turned. "I need to get organized and prepare to leave. I will see you later."

Licia nodded, head spinning as the door closed. And here she thought things were settled and going along smoothly!

XXVI

The quiet in her office almost overwhelmed Licia.

She didn't want to go: hop on a train. To where? For how long? To do what?

She didn't want to stay: She could learn and make contacts in the animal community if she went. Plus there was important work to be done, she thought, out there.

She didn't want to abandon horses to a miserable military fate: They at least deserved decent treatment on the way to war, even if she couldn't stop their use overseas.

And she didn't want to have to choose which person, which man, to be with.

Similar thoughts were running through other's minds as well.

Gace appeared at the door, walked in.

"Licia. Please don't go. What about your work? Your family? Sweet Lightning? She has gotten used to your riding her regularly again. You'll break her heart!

And what about me? Us? Why do you want to throw it all over? Just to ride a train east with a potential saboteur?"

"He's not a war criminal, Gace."

"Not yet, but there is an ember of rage in his heart and who knows what happens when it bursts into flame?"

"You have a point, Gace. But I feel for him. And I want to see how the horses are treated. I don't know what to do."

"You feel for him. Great God, we all feel for the innocents displaced, killed, hurt by that war. Is that a reason to toss away your life and go on a train ride?

"Maybe not, I just am not sure."

He smiled. "I can agree with that."

They looked at each other, thinking. Gace broke the silence.

"Why don't you and I go with him. For a while. Far enough to see the handling and British practices. But then come back. I don't want to get involved with this Pearson character. It sounds like he does some things that, well, that won't stand the light of day. And he clearly wants to draw Cope into his orbit."

A weight came off her shoulders. "Yes. That will give us a chance to learn and meet people and observe. But I promise we will steer clear of taking action."

GACE AND LICIA ARRANGED TO BE GONE FOR A WEEK OR TEN days. Cope packed up, intending to leave Colorado for good. He telegraphed Pearson.

> Leaving with next trainful from Cheyenne stop Will advise when I leave stop Bringing two associates stop What will I be doing in nola stop Oursa

He got a response within hours.

Come alone rpt alone stop Tell friends nothing stop Will advise tasks in person only stop Pearson

---

COPE DISOBEYED, AND SHOWED THEM PEARSON'S 'GRAM. GACE shrugged.

"I don't really want to know details. Licia and I are going along only so far. We want to see how the horses and mules are treated. And scope out the British facilities down there. What you cook up later with other people is your game, not ours."

Cope nodded. "Fair enough. Gace, what does your friend Read say about the next shipment?"

"He and I are barely talking. We kind of need to keep the arrangement. The selling and buying needs to go on, but he and I don't like each other. What I'm saying is, I don't really know their schedule."

Licia snorted. "Piers-Read is not a friend. Not to you, me or Gace. He is a military man on a mission. You can bet that he would throw any one of us under the train in a heartbeat if we look like we would harm or delay him."

Cope mimed a military salute, standing at attention. "You got that right, ma'am!"

She smiled, shook her head.

"The good thing is, we don't need him to learn shipment schedules. When we were up there I made a contact in the yards. Very useful, what those guys see. If you want to really know talk to the men on the ground. Anyway, he tells me cars are being prepared to attach to a regular run east, towards Chicago. Looks like the one scheduled to go out the day after tomorrow, at dawn."

"So we'd better get up there by tomorrow evening."

THE EASTERN SKY WAS LIGHTENING. THE SKY WAS CLOUDLESS and soon the sun would peer over the land, making and chasing shadows.

"Gace, thank you for taking care of the tickets. Three sleepers in the same car is a good arrangement."

Licia smiled. Gace and Cope exchanged shaded glances, wondering just who it would be a good arrangement for.

She went on. "The horses are not crowded in the cars. There are only eight or ten horses or mules per, from what I saw. By the way I didn't see Piers-Read, although I did see officer types supervising the loading. My contact said there are three or four men who do that."

"I heard," Gace said," that he left yesterday to New York for a meeting. He'll not bother us on this trip."

"All aboard!" They were in or near seats and the conductor's cry didn't cause them to move. There was the normal jerking and clanking as the engineer applied power and movement started. Not but a few minutes they were out of town and scudding across the prairie.

"It is a downhill run from here clear to the Missouri River!" The conductor announced this as he walked the aisle answering questions and tucking in the stray loose end.

Cope looked out, comparing the high plains of Wyoming and Nebraska to the veld at home. Then came images of burning barns and riderless horses. He shuddered and pulled the shade. 'Damn,' he thought. 'I sure wish I was already in

New Orleans and working with Pearson on something to hurt the Engelse.'

GENERAL PEARSON SAT AT A DESK. THE NEWS FROM THE AFRIkaaner front was not good. They were slowly being overwhelmed. Those not killed were relocated to camps and towns. The Boers were running out of men and out of options.

He vaguely listened to an aide making a report. "The judge will likely not give us a hearing on our Neutrality Act challenge. We need to have other plans if that happens."

Pearson wouldn't have said that but his assistant did, and the man was right. The guy was about five feet tall, muscled and wide. He answered to Squot and was a fireball who said what he thought. Which is why Pearson kept him around. The little guy continued speaking truth to power.

"We need to stop the ships the British are using to move horses."

The General put up his hands. "You may be right, Squot. But I don't, we can't, be a part of that. The sheriff would love to use the Neutrality Act against us."

His aide just gazed at him, saying nothing.

Pearson paused, thinking, looking to and fro around the room. He came to a decision, looked his man in the eye. "As an officer and head of a branch of the Boer Army we can't take the fight to the enemy in a third nation. That just won't work. But… If someone were to dream up some way on their own, well, hell, who could stop them? It is a big world."

The Squot man looked hard at his boss, for probably a full minute. He then nodded, turned and left.

Licia was a little tired of riding the train. Missouri and Illinois were as boring as a Russian novel.

"Why are we stopping? Aren't we due in Chicago soon?" The conductor eyed the young woman traveling with two men.

"Horse exercise stop. We are on a siding and every horse or mule on board will be taken off and exercised. Any dead ones will be removed. The lame and halt likely shot."

"Shot?!"

"Yes. If they can't be easily treated and healed, no point in prolonging their pain. We do this every twenty four hours. Make a stop, exercise and cull the animals."

"Oh?"

"Yes. At tomorrow's cull stop, the train will separate. The passengers and most freight will go on to Chicago. The horse cars will attach to a run heading down the Mississippi, to Louisiana."

She pulled out her ticket and looked. "It looks like I am booked to go with the horses. Is that right?"

He glanced. "Yes ma'am. You'll go not go through to Chicago but be in a car attached to go to NOLA. New Orleans."

Down by the Gulf, the heat was unlike Denver's sunny dryness. Even the humidity just before a mountain thunderstorm was just a waft of dampness compared to the steamy air—or was it dry steam—that passed for lung fuel in New Orleans.

Licia wondered. "How is it that people' lungs aren't scorched and drowned at the same time? This heat and moisture are thick."

"True that. And it isn't just the lungs. I have seen a groady skin condition on some animals." Gace shook his head. "Not sure if it is a rash or a fungus. Those poor horses need some high plains time to dry out, not time in a ship's hold then Africa."

"Have you seen a lot? Of this, this 'groadiness'?"

"Nah. Out of all the, what, hundred or so corrals the Brits keep at Chalmette, I only saw three or four cases. Conditions there seem clean and well managed, I have to say."

She nodded. "That's my impression as well. Plus, a colleague from the New York CPS office was recently here. Just last month in fact. She told me the Royal Army's holding pens weren't a bad place a month or so ago. They seem to be taking good care of their herds."

Gace sat, steepled his hands, rested his chin on the tip. "From here by train to the docks and onto ships. I wonder how the four legged soldiers like that. Maybe some day I can accompany a freighter on a run. See how the horses I sell from a Colorado ranch fare at sea. And on shore at the other end."

"Now Gace. We agreed we'd go back to Colorado together." She wiped her brow.

"My lord, I have sweated gallons today. And that is while doing nothing strenuous! We'll likely be leaving soon, won't we?" She fanned herself to no avail. "It can't be too soon for me. Especially now that we have seen the layout and procedures. And since Cope has left us to join up with his Mister, or should I say General, Pearson."

"Yeah, he sent a telegram to his general Pearson at the last stop, asking for instructions. He said the answer was kind of fuzzy and he wasn't sure what to do. Hope his trip is worth it and he can do something to hit back at the Engelse. It'd be too bad if he gets stood up or given some simple job any warm body could handle. In any case, we likely have seen the last of him. Too bad, we were getting used to each other, almost like friends. I feel for him."

He took her shoulders and looked her in the eye. "But don't worry, I won't jump on a ship. I was just thinking about how to expand my bragging rights, is all."

"Bragging rights? What?"

"Yeah, I know. Who thinks a guy with horse manure on his boots has anything to brag about, right? Fact is, not one of my competitors has come this far to see how the animals they sell are treated. Hell, most of them haven't even been as far east as Chicago. This trip, what I have learned and what I can now confidently talk on, will be good for my business. Going overseas sometime in the future will be too."

Licia rolled her eyes. "Let me see those boots, pardner!"

A smiling Gace stepped back and half lifted a boot for her to see. "Don't worry, Leesh, you and I are going home, two or three days at the latest. We will get out of this city with a wet sponge to breathe from."

"Good." She smiled, but her tone turned serious. "And when you do go overseas you better take me along."

Cope read and reread the telegram from Pearson.

> Glad you here stop Go building forty seven by the docks stop Report to Squot stop He speaks for me follow instructions to the letter stop Pearson

The Afrikaaner was deflated. So he had come clear across the country just to meet some dope assistant down at the dockyards? He was of half a mind to throw it all off and return west with Gace and Licia.

An image of a burning barn and his mother being marched away at bayonet point seared his brain. Even thinking of quitting now made him ashamed. So he stuffed the 'gram in a pocket and decided he need a drink. He headed towards the waterfront. He wanted to see where this building 47 was, and what he might expect.

The bar faced a deck. It was fairly well lit and not too grungy. He had been in worse.

"What'll you have, mister?" The dark haired man had olive skin, eyes alert for trouble, and his smile seemed pasted on, not friendly.

"A beer."

The barman popped a top and clanked the bottle down. "Twenty five cents. Or do you want to run a tab?"

"Tab. Say, what kind of goods get shipped out of this place?"

"You're new here aren't you?"

"Yeah. Been out in Colorado but decided to make a change. Just got here."

"Well, New Orleans" he said it like 'nawlins,' not two words, "ships out—and ships in—anything man can make or want. You name it, it goes through here. From pecans to machinery to bulk cement to people, any and everything gets moved through this port."

"Jobs? Think I can find a job on the docks? I like animals. Anyone shipping animals?"

The man served another patron and returned.

"Hell yes. Jobs are there for anyone willing to work. Animals? The Army is sending horses to Cuba and other places in Central America. The British are sending gobs of horses out to somewhere, I think Africa. I guess I should say herds of horses, not gobs. I'm a city boy from the delta, not a Colorado cowboy! And I hear that some traders are moving cattle too, but I'm not too sure about that."

Cope indicated he wanted one more. Cold wet beer hit the spot.

The man served him. "Say, my brother knows the business. I know he has handled some shipments of animals. He works in building 46, across and down the street. His name is Robert. Tell him I sent you. I'm San, short for Sandoval."

They shook hands. "I'm Cope, short for Copernicus. Thanks, I'll go see Robert in building 46."

Cope finished his beer and left. He wasn't sure if he would call on Robert or not. But he sure was going to scout out building 47 which had to be nearby.

XXVII

Gace and Licia took the time to enjoy New Orleans' architecture and other unique opportunities.

He looked at a guidebook. "This city was started in 1718 by the French. The eastern colonies, the British ones up north, were just getting established then. Lots of history here."

"Yes. I myself have seen enough of three story overhanging buildings with iron rails. They are rusted like crazy. And the narrow streets give me claustrophobia. I like being able to see a ways, which you can't here. While we're here I suppose we may as well see what the area has to offer. But another day or two of this will be enough. When are we leaving, Gace?"

"Well, the private cabins aren't easy to reserve. Soonest I could get was three days from now. Maybe we take a boat down to the sea one day. That'd be interesting."

"Plus it might get us a breeze. Let's do that."

"I'll try for tomorrow or the day after, Leesh. Let's go try some Cajun food."

Cope ambled out of the bar, stopped. He studied the numbers on the street and turned towards where he expected building forty seven. Soon it appeared. He wondered about this man Squot. And why Pearson wasn't willing to meet him.

He went in. There wasn't a lobby, just a big room. There were chairs around haphazardly, a few occupied. A man looked him over like a side of beef.

"Help you?" His accent was familiar. Cope guessed the man was an Boer.

Without thinking, he replied in Afrikaaner.

"I'm here to see Squot. Pearson sent me."

The man jumped up, got in Cope's face. His speech was heavily accented and the words were in American.

"Don't speak that tongue. There are many British around." He stopped and twice rolled his eyes towards at a few men across the room who were idling, apparently ignoring the two of them. He muttered softly. "Englisher seamen. And they listen and they talk. So, we want no Boer talk, you hear!? And no talk of whoever it was sent you, got it?"

Cope stepped back, nodded, muttered back. "Are there a lot of those limey dogs around?"

"Yah. They're crewmen on one of the ships taking horses over there."

Images of flame overtook him and he took half a step. He couldn't help it, he wanted to swing and kick and start to get even. The guy sensed it. He put his hand lightly on Cope's elbow. "I understand. Don't. Now, you wanted to see Squot, right?

"Yah."

His tone and expression hardened, almost inquisitorial. "What's your name? Where you from? And when did you get here?"

Cope figured he was on the bubble. He could gain entry or find himself swimming—or sinking—in the Mississippi. He looked the guy in the eye and answered, straightforward and quick. In American.

The man listened carefully. He stared for half a minute, the silence roaring in Cope's ears. The man relaxed as he reached a decision. Holding his hand out, he smiled.

"I'm Squot. The man told me to expect you, Cope. Come on, let's walk." He strode for the door. Cope caught up and they walked along the pier, two among many.

"How can you stand to be in the same room with those Engelse? Why there of all places?"

Squot chuckled. "I daydream about hurting some of them. But really, parking in their living barracks and offices is smart. How better to know what the enemy is up to? To them I am just a dumb immigrant. Looking for work. I do nothing to change that. The more I fade into the background the more I learn. Which ships are coming and going, when they are leaving, and so on."

He stopped and faced Cope. "Remember that. Hard as it is, you have to keep your head down and mouth shut. Give them nothing to remember you by, no dirty looks, nothing. Do you understand? Will you do it that way?"

"Yah. Don't like it but I'll do it."

"Good. Because if you don't, if you cause trouble, you'll have to answer to them. And after they're done, you'll have to deal with me and Pearson. Believe me, you do not want that."

Cope held up his hands in mock surrender.

"Hey, I get it. I want to hurt the Engelse but not us or you or me. You tell me what to do and I'll do it, and nothing more."

They resumed walking. Squot nodded and then was quiet, thinking, then blurted. "We need to stop the ships. Need to stop one for the whole world to see."

"Sounds right to me, Squot. What can I do?"

Squot's gaze seemed to go through him, measuring his soul.

"You can help us stop one." He looked around, leaned in and whispered. "The man picked one. It is General Pearson's ship. That's the one he wants done." Squot leaned back and resumed talking as he had been. "Especially if we can block the harbor or channel with it. Not one full of horses. Can you do that?"

"I have a press pass. Could probably get aboard a ship. But I know nothing about stopping or anything about ships. Explosives? No idea. What…?"

"Not sure exactly to go about it. We want to hit an empty one. No point in sinking a ship full of horses. Troops, yes but not animals. Still, if you can get aboard you can carry a suitcase." He stopped so Cope did too. He grinned. "We will provide one to you, a suitcase or bag. It will be loaded with explosives and a timer. Get it down below somehow. We can make it easy for you to arm, to set the timer. That should do it."

Cope thought aloud. "You make it sound so easy. What do I do if I am able to get on board, plant and arm a bomb? Then do I jump in the river? Sacrifice myself? Huddle in a safe place and hope for the best?"

Squot again stopped, faced Cope. "You can probably just saunter off, leave. We'll try to have a rowboat left nearby if you have to jump and swim for it. No promises on that; we'll try. But you need to know, remember, that officially we do not know you or anything about you. Whatever happens, you are on your own with this." He waited. "Shall we go ahead and get a bag ready?"

"We? What do you mean we? You say I'll be alone, Mister Squot."

"We. You will have support. We will aid you in every way but public acknowledgment, or help if you are caught. So." Squot's smile was maniacal. "Just don't get caught."

XXVIII

Cope paused, took in the crazy grin, and then spoke.

"So let me recap the deal. I will risk my life carrying a bomb on board and setting it. And then risk it by trying to get off the boat. And you will provide a cheering section who turn their backs if I get caught."

"It is a ship not a boat. The SS Pamplona, a British owned stock carrier, will arrive tomorrow. She's scheduled to be…"

"She?"

"Cope, if you want to fit in you need to talk the talk. Ships are always referred to in the feminine. Not an it, not a boat, but a she."

"Oh. Sorry, I am no seaman, just a dumb Boer farmer."

"Well don't act like one. Get with it if you want to help us."

Cope nodded and stiffly replied. "You were saying *she* is scheduled to arrive when? Tomorrow?"

"Yes. The Pamplona is coming up from the delta now, as we speak. She's due to dock early tomorrow. Then she undergoes a day of light maintenance, cleaning and coaling. A reduced crew will stay on board. They intend to load her with horses day after tomorrow and then she's off to Africa."

"So, tomorrow during the maintenance work is the day to do our job. My job."

Cope looked at Squot, who smiled. "Yes, you go get the job done tomorrow. Bring it all home tomorrow after dark if you can."

"Bring it home? Oh, I see, make it happen then."

"Yup. Not bad for a dumb Boer farmer."

"If I can find a way, I'll have her take a few Engelse down with her."

Squot beamed, pleased. He nodded.

"Tell you what, we'll have you carry a toolbag not a suitcase. Same thing, same contents as a suitcase. But it'll fit in better. A toolbag carried on board a ship being cleaned won't attract attention like a suitcase would. I'll arrange things for you. Pick it up any time after noon tomorrow. At building 47. When you do, you are Alex, not Cope. The handoff will go to Alex, got it?"

"With all the Engelse there?"

"Yes. We want to look like it is just a normal day, a normal pick up. Nothing sly or unusual about it. As far as they know you will be just another dumb tradesman going to work for them. Whenever we can, we take advantage of their arrogance and their sense of invulnerability. Good luck, Cope. Or should I say, Alex?"

The shook hands and parted.

COPE WANDERED THE DOCKS. HE FELT DAZED AND EXCITED and apprehensive. He sat on a bench, watched ships and men and cranes moving cargo. So it was finally happening. He could at last strike a blow for his country and its citizens.

He exulted at that. Then it occurred to him that this could be his last night on earth. Would he pull off a sinking, maybe killing Engelse for his father? That would be good. But better would be to do that, get off the boat and live to somehow do it again. He wryly thought Squot would encourage him to get off the ship not the boat. He felt alone; decided to go somewhere he could be with people.

LICIA AND GACE SPENT THE DAY ON A SMALL STEAMER. It was more or less a water cab running between New Orleans' docks and the far reaches of the delta. The Mississippi River ran for another hundred or so miles before it spent itself in the Gulf of Mexico. The boat had stopped at many settlements along the river, but they were glad to be nearing the pier and be back in the city.

Gace stopped a crew member. "What's a good seafood restaurant nearby? For us northern travelers? We'll be returning home soon and would like an evening on the waterfront."

"When you come off the ship, turn right and go a block. There are two or three good ones in that stretch. Menus are displayed outside so you can pick and choose. You can't go wrong there."

Licia remarked on the day. "That was interesting for the first stop or two. Those little fishing villages all started to look pretty much alike after that." Coming off the gangplank, they turned right and headed towards the restaurants.

"Yeah. In a way they reminded me of small mountain towns. Each place has a store, a tavern, an inn, separate or all in one building, and a few houses. Maybe a church and a school. The people seemed to know everyone around."

Licia laughed. "And they looked at us outsiders as either crooks or fools to be separated from their money."

He chuckled, nodded. "And gad, the mosquitoes. This country is not for me. The sooner we—hey, there's Cope! Coming down the street towards us."

"Cope, hello! Cope!?"

Lost in thought, Cope at first didn't hear the greeting.

"Oh, hello. Sorry, was daydreaming. I thought you two were already on the train halfway back to Colorado. What are you doing, still here?"

"How about we talk about it over dinner?"

Later, Licia gently pushed the plate away.

"That was surprisingly good. Before this trip I thought of crawfish as the icky little crawdads in the irrigation ditches and creeks. Not almost shrimp sized cuisine material. Dessert, anyone?

They ordered from the cart, and soon were enjoying.

Licia's curiosity took over. "So, Cope, we parted ways up north before the train stopped to disgorge its horses at the Chalmette corrals. You kind of disappeared. Where'd you go and what have you been doing since?"

Gace nudged her knee under the table. His mutter was loud enough for both to hear. "Or maybe we don't want to know?"

Cope smiled. "Oh, this and that. How about you?"

"We saw the set up at Chalmette. You no doubt saw it too but we got a tour of the place. The Brits have that down to a science. They sort and check the animals on arrival. If care is needed the horse is taken care of. Only strong and healthy ones are put aboard ships."

Cope looked between the two of them, obviously weighing his words.

"Oh? And do they shoot the lame ones like they did along the trip east?"

"No, and the conductor told me that was unusual. Most of the time they heal the horse up if they can. That's what they do there, at Chalmette. They treat the sick ones, get them healthy for the voyage. Only the incurable or gravely injured, like a broken leg, are put down."

Cope's smile was frosty. "Well, you're right, Licia. I did get to see it. Chalmette. And it made me sick. All those animals, going into the dark cold holds of ships to cross the Atlantic. Tied in a stall for weeks, unable to move. The Atlantic is a rough passage for any ship. And then the survivors will face battle. And be used to kill my people."

"Oh Cope. We can't stop the British Empire. Or wars."

He stood. "No? Maybe they can't be stopped but they sure can be slowed. This is the place to do it. I have made some friends and will be staying here. Our struggle against the British will continue."

He looked away, almost contentedly. "So far I've only been able to use words against 'em. But now maybe I have some other weapons."

The gaze hardened, focused. He shrugged. "I really should go. Tomorrow will be a big day."

Before leaving, he looked at his friends. "You may want to watch the newspapers the next few days."

Licia held out a hand as if to stop him. "If you need us or anything, we're at the hotel Grand."

AFTER HE LEFT, THE TWO LOOKED AT EACH OTHER.

"New friends? 'Our' struggle, not 'my' struggle? I wonder who he has gotten tied up with. Probably that Pearson character."

"I don't know," Licia frowned. "But he talked like something will happen tomorrow."

"Well, I guess we'll find out then. Feels to me like he has washed his hands of us. Still, I'm glad you told him where we are, just in case. But I have to say, God only knows what he may be up to."

"I'm tired. We have no small day tomorrow ourselves. Need to finish packing, pick up train tickets, get ready to go home. What time does the train leave?"

"Tomorrow night late. Let's go back to the hotel."

THE COUPLE LOOKED AROUND THE WATERFRONT BEFORE THEY climbed into the carriage back to the hotel. Ships came and went, tug boats scurried, men talked and cursed, cranes screeched. Coal smoke and haze hung low.

"This seems confusion, but I guess freight and people get safely on board and moved along." Gace ran a hand through his hair. "Boy, it looks like any small snag could cause big problems in a harbor like this. But what does a Colorado cowboy know? No doubt they know what they're doing."

"Get in, Gace. Let's go. It is late and I am tired." Licia herself scanned around the scene. She didn't register a person standing in a shadow by the restaurant, watching them watch the waterfront.

Cope smiled at Gace's remark. 'You hit the nail on the head, my friend. Small snag indeed! You just wait and see!' After the carriage left, he slipped away.

XXIX

The next day went in fits and starts, alternately crawling then careening.

Licia and Gace packed up.

"I can't believe we bought this much stuff! Look at that—no way it'll go in our luggage."

"Yes, it is quite a haul of souvenirs and gifts. I guess we'd better go buy another case to carry it all in."

"Let's have a nice luncheon or early dinner as well. Who knows when we can have fresh seafood again."

Later, a new suitcase having been bought and packed, they went out. The couple strolled the waterfront before choosing a restaurant.

"This has been a pleasant and worthwhile trip. I learned a lot."

Gace smiled. "Yeah, I saw new things and places, met folks and so on. But to me, the company is what made it special."

"Yes, Gace, I agree. I enjoyed spending this time with you." Her tone changed. "I wouldn't feel bad about spending more."

Gobsmacked but pleased, he didn't know what to say. He was tongue tied, couldn't think a good answer. To his chagrin she went on.

"Speaking of company, I have to say I am concerned about Cope. His attitude and his actions."

Gace was relieved in a way even though he had missed an opportunity. At least this was a safe, un-fragile subject to talk on.

 "Yeah. Whatever he is doing, I hope he doesn't land himself in jail or worse. I can't blame the guy for being angry. I'd want to throw a wrench into the works too. Can't imagine seeing see your kin killed and scattered. But still, it does no good at all to get yourself hurt, killed, or jailed."

"So true. It is hard to watch. But enough of Cope. Where do you want to eat?"

"Wherever you are, Leesh. I want to spend more time with you." He took a chance, and added, "too."

WHILE LICIA AND GACE FRETTED, PACKED, AND FLIRTED, Cope slept late.

He woke rested. The sun fought through haze and humidity. The bright globe was, a rare sight on the lower Mississippi. Lazing in bed, he watched patterns of sun and shade dapple the wall.

Stretching his arms, he visualized going on board the Pamplona. He looked like just another worker and would have no trouble getting there. And then placing the explosives filled toolbag. Where would it do most damage? Should it be next to a boiler, if he could get it there? Or the main electrical panel? Maybe just the side of the boat…Ship, he reminded himself. Put it on the side away from the pier, the outboard side. That way if it capsized it might clog up the harbor. If he placed it near the galley maybe he could kill a few crewmen along with sinking the damn boat. Ship. How could he get the captain? Wouldn't that be a coup, kill the captain and sink his boat. Ship. Maybe he should take a pistol in case he had to fight his way off. Or should he just sit down next to the toolbag and let it do its work?

From that gleeful brainstorm, his mind turned. He saw his father being shot. The man was just out on commando astride his horse, trying to protect his way of life. And some son of a dog Engelse killed him. To this day Cope didn't know details. He just hoped it was quick. And he saw his mother pulling his siblings from a flaming house, watching in horror as soldiers bayoneted their livestock, one by one. And then the family, possessing nothing but the clothes they wore, being marched off to an open air prison.

By then Cope was ready to take that pistol and go shoot the captain. Or any other Engelse he could find. He shook his head. Laying and breathing calmly, he tried and finally got his racing heart to slow. The clock showed ten. He had most of two hours to clean up, shave, and eat. Plenty of time before going to building 47 for his toolbag.

As he enjoyed breakfast he fleetingly wondered if this was his last meal. Pondering that, he found he didn't care. His focus was on exploding the boat. Ship. And killing Engelse in the bargain.

AT BUILDING 47, SQUOT WAS NOWHERE TO BE SEEN. A NON-descript guy seated at a desk stared at him. He could have been any man. He was medium sized, shortish light brown hair, brown eyes, no memorable features or traits. He spoke with a strange but understandable accent. "You Alex? Must be, you match the description. What you here for?"

Cope was terse. "Yeah, I'm Alex. Here for a bag. A special toolbag. Squot said he'd have it ready."

Anyman nodded and reached under the desk. With some difficulty he wrestled out a large carpet bag. Bags like it were used all over the harbor to carry tools, supplies, what have you. Cope had seen identical bags everywhere, toted by all sorts—tradesmen, clerks, even housewives. The bag plonked on the desk and neither spoke, just looked.

"When you're ready, pull on this hard, one time. Tug it pretty good." Anyman pointed but didn't touch a protruding piece of small rope. On looking closer, Cope saw it wasn't rope but was stout string or twine really. "When you do that you should a click or clunk. That means it is armed and will do its business in about seven minutes."

Cope stared, fascinated.

Anyman looked him in the eye, smiled, and confirmed. "Pull once, seven minutes. Got it?"

Using both hands, Anyman held the bag out for Cope. "Good luck, Alex." He turned away.

The bag was kind of heavy and Cope had to grab quick with both hands. He hefted it, slung it on a shoulder and set out.

He walked down the waterfront and found a bench where he could see the SS Pamplona. It was a typical steamer from what he could see. A few streaks of rust colored the sides but all in all she seemed fairly neat and businesslike. There was a big door on the side, probably a ramp for the horses, he guessed. If he could knock that off with his bomb she'd be out of commission. But no, he decided he wanted to sink not harm her. One less horse carrier for the Engelse. And get publicity. He knew Pearson wanted the public eye on the British and their atrocities.

Lost in thought, he didn't see Licia and Gace strolling. Her greeting brought him aware.

She eyed the carpetbag taking up much of the bench.

"Cope! What, are you packed up and ready to leave town? Didn't you tell us you were staying?"

"Oh, uh, I have a job. These are tools I am delivering to a ship here." He pointed. "The SS Pamplona. Just over there. She's one of the fleet of horse carriers for the Engelse."

Gace chuckled. "Tools, huh? Since when did you know a hammer from a drill bit?"

Licia eyed the bag skeptically.

Cope smiled. "I grew up on a farm, far from any town, store, or blacksmith. Out there you have to fix and build things for yourself. You learn how to make do. So yeah, Gace, I know tools." He smiled. "The hammer has those two bent rabbit ear thingies, right?"

"You got it! And the drill bit has a spiral ramp up its length, did you know?"

Licia rolled her eyes. "Tell me, Cope the carpenter, why are you going to help a horse carrier do its job?"

Gace's smile evaporated. "Good point, Leesh." Looking at Cope, he asked, "What gives?"

"Just a quick delivery job. I need to get it on board and set up for the right guy, and I can leave. Nothing much to it." Cope couldn't hide his smirk as he thought of setting the bag below the captain's desk.

"Set up, huh?" Gace eyed the bag and Cope. "Cope, I hope you aren't…"

"Leave me alone! Don't worry about me. I know what I'm doing and I don't need your preaching. Why don't you two just go back to the Rockies and let me be."

With that Cope stood, grabbed the bag, and marched off towards his SS Pamplona.

XXX

THE EASE OF BOARDING WAS SURPRISING. HE SIMPLY NOTED the name, the SS Pamplona. There was her gangplank which he walked right up. It was like he owned the tub, which in a warped way, he did. Once on board, he turned right then left through the first door, or was it called a hatch. He wasn't sure and didn't really care. He felt his ticker racing so fast he was afraid it might burst. Deep breaths helped to slow things down. There was no challenge, no second look. He was just another focused and gainful tradesman.

Greasy, busy men climbed all over the engine room. This was not the place to leave his bag and its message.

"Hey, I'm looking for the electrical room, the main panel." The man he stopped eyed him up and down. Cope's clean clothes stood out and felt a nugget of panic in his gut. The man's answer was sardonic.

"You're an electrician alright. You guys and your clean hands and clothes. As if a bit of grease would hurt things."

Cope smiled, thinking fast. "You don't know the half of it. A bit of grease would hurt things. That stuff is hard on the connectivity of those copper wires. You want lights to come on when you flip a switch, don't you? And you don't need a shock when you pull a lever down here. Right?" He didn't know the first thing about electrical connectivity but figured neither did this guy.

The guy grudgingly nodded. "Yah, I guess. The main electrical station is down two decks and up forward." He jerked his thumb to indicate a direction.

'Down and up,' Cope mused as he walked the indicated direction. He sure was glad he didn't have to work in such a topsy turvy place, and the sooner he could deposit the bag and get off, the better. The whole thing gave him the willies.

He worked his way down to the next deck. The hold, the area with individual stalls for the horses, was quiet. He noticed slings and blankets. Would the animals be tied in, unable to move for weeks? What a miserable time that would be for them! He went on down, determined to sink the damn thing or at least make sure it couldn't haul horses for quite a while.

Near as he could tell he was on the deck with water just outside, the lowest on the boat. Ship. What did Squot call that lowest deck? The oarlock? No, that held the paddle on a rowboat. The orlop, that was it! He was on the orlop deck, he hoped.

He took a moment to orient himself, looking around trying to find a landmark. Or would it be a shipmark? Was he down and up, lower deck at the front? He shook his head to get rid of such nonsense, and started. He was going forward, as best he could tell. Wandering around down in the bowels of the Pamplona, it was hard to keep things straight. The thought came again, there was no way he could be a sailor, living in a giant machine. Cope stuffed a longing for the freedom and openness of the sun drenched, breezy veld, his beloved African prairie.

He went through an opening to another compartment. It was guarded by a big door which could be closed and locked by turning a big wheel which looked like the spoked ship's steering wheel. He wondered why such armor was needed deep in the ship, but realized he really didn't care.

On the other side of the big wheeled door, there was a locker, up against the side. The size was ideal: about four feet by four feet and two feet deep. It was half full of small boxes. The locker door was open and it flopped lazily with the gentle movement of the Pamplona. Its hinges squeaked with every flop. Alone, he stopped and listened. Grabbing the door to silence it, he made sure he heard no one nearby. The quiet was creepy and he tried not to think that he was standing well below the waterline. Cope decided this was the place. He couldn't wait for vengeance.

Into the locker went the bag. Apparently the boxes were empty or only half full, since the bag crushed them. They collapsed with a sigh. Cope made sure the bag was sitting stably, adjusting a few boxes. Then he took a deep breath, held the bag firm with one hand while the other tugged the twine. Things worked as told—he definitely heard, and felt, a clunk. Closing the locker, Cope looked around for a few seconds. Then hurried up and out into fresh air.

The bomb was set. He fervently hoped that seven minute lag time was accurate. He headed up, longing even more frantically for open space and fresh air. 'There!,' he thought. 'There's the door out to the ramp off this tub!' As he came out into what passed for a sunny day in Louisiana, his face fell.

The gangplank was clogged with a line! Four or five men stood on the gangplank, waiting to get to shore. As many more stood on the deck waiting their turn. He didn't know if it was an end of shift problem, some security check, or what.

Cope grabbed his stomach, moaned loudly, and half staggered, half shouldered his way.

"Sick man coming through," he croaked, trying to look and sound miserable. The man ahead didn't move. He half turned his head, didn't even look, and chuckled sarcastically.

"Tough luck, buddy. We are all sick and ready to get off this bucket. Wait your turn. Puke over the rail if you have to." He turned away, moving ahead a step or two.

Cope slapped his cheeks, leaving a few scratches for good measure. He croaked again. "I wish I was just puking. I have some kind of fever or pox. Look at the red marks!"

The man looked, his eyes got big and he stepped back, hitting the railing.

"Pox! Chicken pox! Small pox! This man is catching!"

He pulled at the man in front of him and they stepped aside. The line disintegrated as people got out of the way of the infected one. Cope staggered down the plank, lowering his face and putting a protective arm up. In a moment he was close to the shore, the pier.

There was a tremendous 'whump.' The Pamplona rocked as if picked up then dropped by Poseidon. Smoke poured out her side and she started to shake and settle. The gangplank fell; Cope and others went in to the river.

AT ABOUT THAT TIME, HIS FRIENDS WERE PART WAY ACROSS town. They were just on the train, starting the trip back west. The train station was as usual chaotic noisy and smoky. The train started with a lurch causing Licia's shoulder to bump Gace. She smiled and half chanted, half sang a rhythmic farewell.

"So long, Nawlins. Glad I met ya but your swamps and bugs and rain and crowds are too much for me."

Gace smiled. "Me too. This trip was worthwhile but it'll be good to be home. We ought to be in St Louis for breakfast. Then we catch a connection and head west."

"Yes, we're scheduled into Denver tomorrow late." Licia looked around, watching as they left the river behind. "I imagine that pretty soon the attendant will come make up our beds."

As if on cue, a slender, uniformed man came in. His skin was ebony, eyes blue. She still had to listen carefully to hear the meaning of the words spoken in thick Cajun accent. "Are you ready, ma'am, to have the sleeper made up? I can come by later if you want."

He glanced at Gace as if gaining permission to chat.

"Now is fine. We'll head to the dining car."

The attendant nodded. "Alright suh, ma'am. I will get after it. Say, did youall hear about the ship?"

The couple looked at each other. Gace asked, "What ship? What happened?"

He ran his hand over his shaved head, an anxious expression on his face. "An explosion at a ship at dock. Or I guess it was at dock but was about ready to move over to be loaded up. It is a horse hauler ship, my friend told me."

"Explosion! On a ship? A horse hauler? Which ship? Was it sunk? People hurt?"

"Suh, I do not know about that. She was named the Pamela, or was it the Pampong? Something like that. I do not know if anyone was hurt. If there was an explosion I expect someone was, maybe someone killed. Don't know. She was not sunk but is badly damaged I hear."

Licia blurted. "The Pamplona."

"Yes ma'am, that's the name, the Pamplona! Word is, she is burning and adrift, damaged. She will not be hauling any horses soon. But not sunk." He rubbed his head again and glanced into the compartment. "Now, if youall are going to dinner I can make the beds up while you are gone."

Gace and Licia said nothing until they were seated and had ordered.

"Well, Leesh, quite the news, isn't it? Now we know what kind of 'tools' were in that bag."

"You may be right, Gace." She paused. "You probably hit the nail on the head."

As he rolled his eyes, she smiled. "Pun intended."

Then she looked around to see if anyone was listening, and softly said, "I hope Cope is…alright."

"He's likely a hunted man now. Maybe he got away. And he is alive and unhurt. In either case, God help him."

THE LIGHTS WERE ON IN THE OFFICES OF BOER ARMY GENERAL Samuel Pearson. They were often burning and people were working late into the night, and this day was no exception.

Pearson was reading a just delivered copy of an extra edition of the newspaper. He shook it, straightening out a page.

"Look at this, Squot. Explosion on a ship! A limey horse hauler! Police think someone set off a bomb. Too bad for the SS Pamplona. It was not loaded at the time, fortunately for the horses."

"So I hear, General. I understand there is a fire, and a new hole in the side. I hear some of the crew were injured. No one killed outright but there are people missing. So my friends on the dock tell me. And like you say, best of all, there were no horses. And the ship is of no use to the British now or for the next few months."

Pearson laughed. "I am glad to see the British get a bloody nose. I wonder if Bill Haywood has heard about this? The mine union boss out in Colorado? He'd love to hear that the big guys took a punch for a change. I think I may send him a letter. Cut the article out so I can send it along."

Squot nodded, although he wasn't a secretary and detested such tasks. Pearson continued.

"I hate to think someone innocent was hurt. If a sailor got hit, well, those who work for the Crown get what they deserve. Maybe this will make the Brits rethink their practice of buying horses here in America. I doubt it but it feels good to see them take a knock."

"Quite, General."

Pearson could off hand think of several men who would have been happy to set a bomb, anywhere. He didn't really need or want to know, but asked anyway. "I wonder who did it? Set the bomb?"

He arched an eyebrow as he asked this.

"I can't imagine, sir." Both smiled knowingly. Squot went on.

"There are plenty of people around who don't like what the limeys are doing. Not only over in South Africa but other parts of their precious 'empah.' Many of them, I would think, would be happy to act with just a little push." His smile broadened. "Matter of fact…"

Pearson rustled the newspaper, pretended to read it. "I don't have time now to speculate on current events, Squot. I need to prepare with the lawyers for our Neutrality Act lawsuit. Guessing about these day to day happenings gets in the way of important things." He smiled. "But we'll take help anywhere we can get it, don't you agree?"

The telegram lay crumpled on the desk. Anger and disgust flooded Major Paul Piers-Read. And questions. What kind of security did the port have? Apparently, none since someone could waltz onto a ship at berth and plant a bomb. Why didn't the ship or the port keep lists of qualified, approved workers? Why or how was it general knowledge that the Pamplona was a horse carrier for the Royal Army? Was anyone of competence monitoring 'General' Pearson and his raggedy band of troublemakers?

Damn, he thought, if he was in charge down there he'd get some answers. He stood, paced, reflecting on events. All in all, he realized, this was nothing. No more harmful than a mosquito bite, a jostle in a busy hallway, or a hostile stare. Royal Army purchasing operations would go on as planned.

Picking up the telegram, he smoothed and reread it. His new secretary, an American, came in. Piers-Read knew he held a reserve commission in the US Army. He suspected but didn't know that the man reported on all he saw at work. Thus, Piers-Read was careful to let the man in only on information he wanted the Americans to know. He waved the telegram.

"Well, bad news."

"Oh? What's that? I usually see the telegrams and tell you, Sir." He smiled to cover his dismay. "Not the other way around."

The Major scowled. "This one came personal to me. Some maniac set off a bomb on one of our horse carriers in New Orleans. She is not sunk, but badly damaged. Some crew injured, some missing. No confirmed fatalities. And no horses on board."

"I agree, that is not good news, Sir. Not sunk and no horses to the positive at least. I'm sure the Louisiana authorities are investigating."

The Major drew himself up as if about to bow to the Queen. "This attempt to murder British merchant sailors and sink our ships is cowardly and shameful. Whoever did it must be brought to justice."

"You can be certain that the New Orleans police are working hard to do just that, Sir."

The British officer went on, ignoring his aide. "But one ship temporarily harmed is a drop in the bucket. We will continue to supply horses and mules to the Royal Army. And we will prevail against the Boers."

XXXI

Cope sidled along the plank, waiting for something, he didn't know what. The force, the noise, the suddenness of the explosion was unexpected and savage. The concussion was like a bull headbutting him in the chest. The gangplank fell. He didn't know if it came off the pier or off the ship. Either way, it dumped him and several others into the Mississippi. One man bounced off the rail and landed square on Cope's back, pushing him well under water. He fought the guy off and surfaced, gasping. People still on deck, those who could, ran away from the smoke and the hole in the side of the ship. Several bodies lay on the deck, some writhing and some still. The crowd on shore gaped.

Wet heavy clothes dragged at Cope. He looked around, spotted a ladder built into the pier. With effort he dog paddled over and climbed up. On the upper rungs, it felt like the Mississippi was tugging him back, not wanting to give him up. Glad to finally be on dry land, he slowly stood erect and looked at the smoking and burning Pamplona.

"Holy cow!" The next man up the ladder stared. For some reason this fellow wore only a pair of trousers, no shirt or shoes. He didn't act chilled, in fact he was worked up and hopping around. It brought to mind something Cope had read about rats in a maze looking agitatedly to escape. The guy was borderline hysterical. "What was that? Was it an explosion? How did it happen? There is a hole in the middle of the ship! Is it sinking?" He turned to Cope. "What happened?"

Cope shook his head. "Don't know. I was on the gangplank trying to get off. I heard a big bang and next thing I knew, I was in the water."

The man calmed a little and looked closer at Cope. "Hey, ain't you the guy with chicken pox or something? The guy who was in such a hurry to get off?"

Stepping close, he grabbed Cope's lapels. "I don't like your accent, fella. You sure were in a tizzy to get off the ship. Did you know something was about to happen? What gives here?" Holding on, he turned back to the ship and yelled. "Hey, this guy knows something! Something about what happened here!"

As the guy squawked, Cope knocked his hands away. Stepping back, he yelled back at his accuser.

"You talk about me! You were trying to get off so fast you ran me over, landed on top of me in the water. What did you know, pal? What were you doing on board? How did you get to the front of the line? If anybody knows something, it is you!" He stepped forward and shoved the shirtless man.

Sirens were coming, from several directions. A group of firemen dragging hoses and pulling hand operated pumps charged down the pier. Some uniformed cops showed up and started moving the crowd away from the fire.

One cop with chevrons on his sleeve yelled out. "Everyone stay here. We need to talk to all witnesses. All of you, every man jack! I repeat, stay on the dock." He then proceeded to blow his whistle and start swinging his billy club.

People started pushing and shoving, arguing, trying to duck the cops. Cope ducked and moved further back. He was able to separate from the melee. Briefly he stopped to assess the damage, what he could see. He hoped the damned boat—ship—would sink but wasn't sure it would. Slipping his wet coat off, he looked like a worker not someone just out of the drink. He looked at the smoke and flame coming from General Pearson's ship, and grinned. Then he looked skyward and quietly said, "Well Dad, we are starting to get even. There will be more."

He edged to near an exit. The police were busy trying to control the crowd and no one was there to stop him. He melted away.

Afterword

THE BRITISH PREVAILED. THEIR SCORCHED EARTH STRATEGY forced Boer leaders to negotiate a surrender. Along the way the Royal Army purchased a quarter of a million horses and mules in the US. About that many were purchased elsewhere around the world.

Ted Moore was the author's grandfather. As an old man he reminisced about the British Army's purchasing commissions often visiting his boyhood home, the Owens Ranch in Byers. Katherine Moore, Ted's mother, managed the ranch. She also filed for and proved up a homestead in the area. Charles Owens sold the ranch not long after this story takes place and retired to Denver. He and Katherine are buried in Crown Hill Cemetery.

Samuel Pearson was a business gadfly, an American citizen. He acted as US liaison for the Boer Army with a title of 'General.' He remained in America, working to ease supply issues and generate publicity for the cause. He once threatened to arm his supporters in order to resist the British on US soil.

A British horse carrier, the SS Mechanization, did in fact suffer an explosion awaiting loading in the New Orleans port. No one took credit but it is believed to be the work of Pearson's sympathizers. She was badly damaged but didn't sink. Pearson's efforts to stop the horse trade via the Neutrality Act failed in a Louisiana Court.

Not long after this story took place, Bill Haywood left the Western Federation of Miners and took up with the International Workers of the World. This labor union, popularly known as the Wobblies, was aggressive and loud in its efforts for its members. Ultimately he left the US for Moscow. The USSR gave him a Hero of Labor medal. He died there in the 1920s and is buried in the Kremlin Wall.

Stay tuned. The McNall brothers continue their adventures.

About the Author

STAN MOORE IS A HUSBAND, FATHER, GRANDFATHER; A THIRD generation Coloradan; an author and historian; a Vietnam veteran; a retired small business owner; and an avid mountaineer, backpacker and desert rat. Moore and his wife make their home near Denver with their cat who lets them stay there.

www.ingramcontent.com/pod-product-compliance
Lightning Source LLC
Chambersburg PA
CBHW030435010526
44118CB00011B/651